D1535806

SOLIDS, STRIPES, CIRCLES, AND SQUARES

16 modern patchwork quilt patterns

PIPPA ECCLES ARMBRESTER

Martingale
Create with Confidence

Solids, Stripes, Circles, and Squares:
16 Modern Patchwork Quilt Patterns
© 2012 by Pippa Eccles Armbrester

Martingale®
19021 120th Ave. NE, Ste. 102
Bothell, WA 98011-9511 USA
ShopMartingale.com

Printed in China
17 16 15 14 13 12   8 7 6 5 4 3 2 1

**Library of Congress Cataloging-in-Publication Data
is available upon request**

ISBN: 978-1-60468-204-5

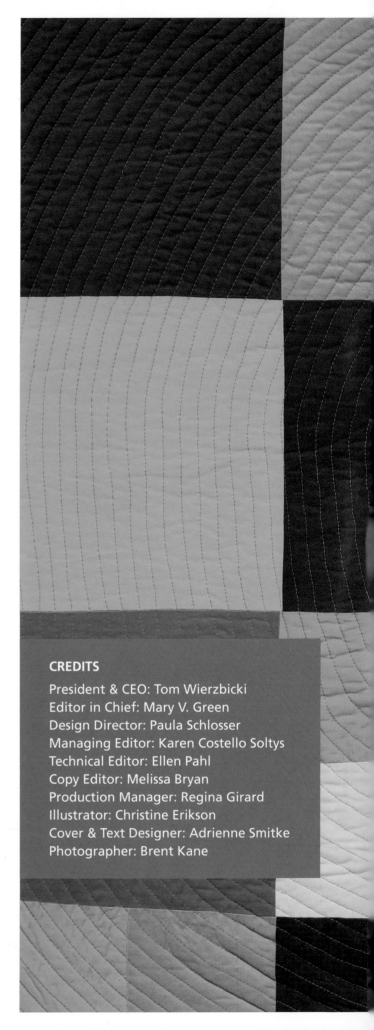

CREDITS

President & CEO: Tom Wierzbicki
Editor in Chief: Mary V. Green
Design Director: Paula Schlosser
Managing Editor: Karen Costello Soltys
Technical Editor: Ellen Pahl
Copy Editor: Melissa Bryan
Production Manager: Regina Girard
Illustrator: Christine Erikson
Cover & Text Designer: Adrienne Smitke
Photographer: Brent Kane

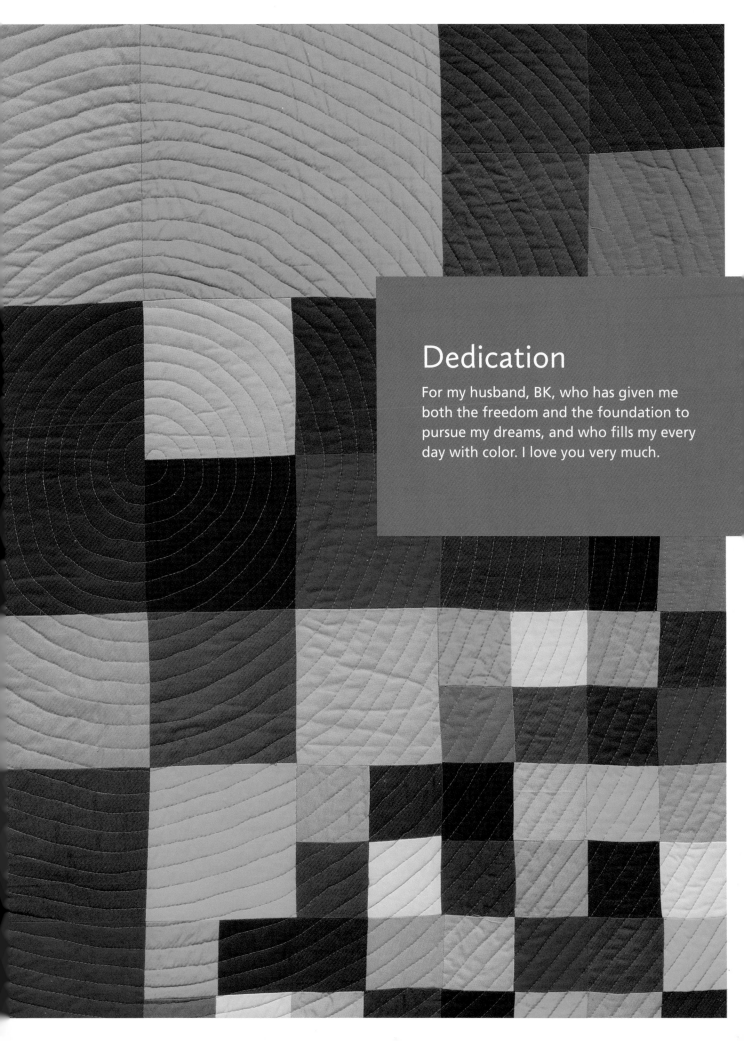

Dedication

For my husband, BK, who has given me both the freedom and the foundation to pursue my dreams, and who fills my every day with color. I love you very much.

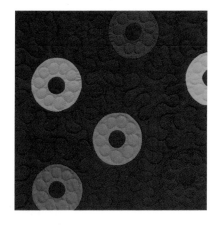

Contents

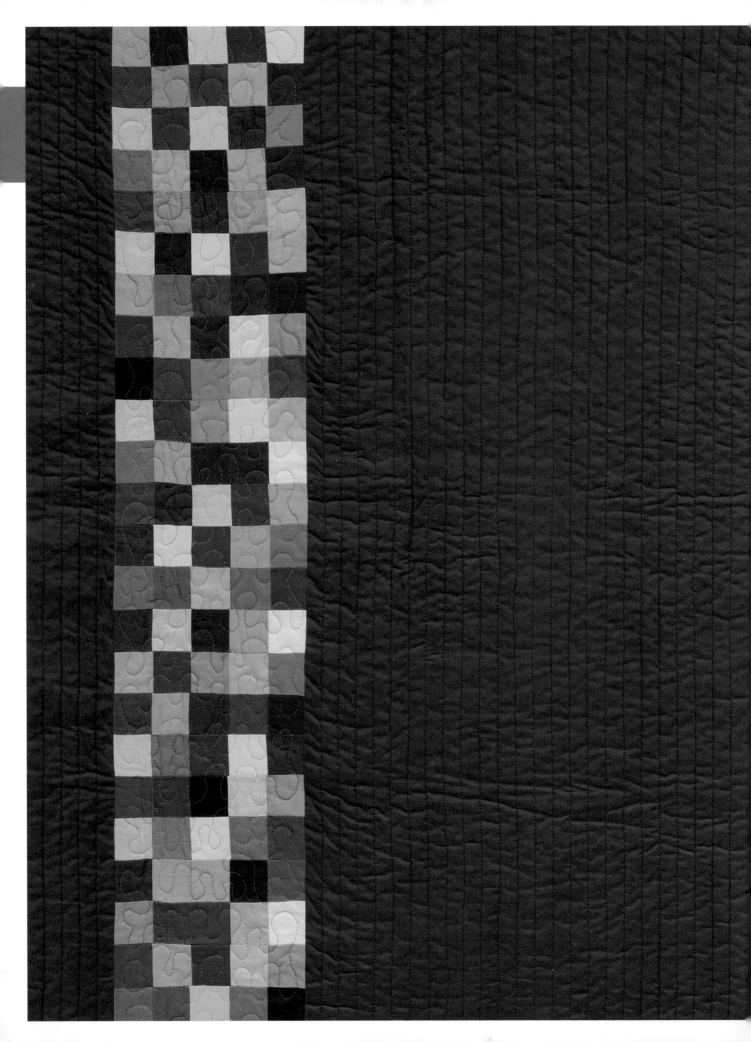

Introduction

I stumbled upon my love of quilting several years ago, and somewhat out of the blue. My grandmother gave me a quilt as a birthday gift while I was a college undergraduate, and having grown up in a crafty and creative family in which everyone was always making something with her hands—from clay figurines to beaded key chains—I was instantly intrigued. I'd done a little sewing here and there in the past, so I decided to give patchwork a try. The obsession was nearly instant. I bought a sewing machine, which I kept on the desk in my dorm room, and amidst studying and paper writing, I would treat myself to bouts of quiltmaking. Something about the process of piecing together fabrics, and the way in which a quilt top functioned as a blank canvas for creativity, satisfied my fondness for both handmade and functional items, and for artistic exploration.

My passion for quilts has been avid and enduring, but like any relationship, it's had some ups and downs as well. The vast world of traditional quilting, combined with the exciting emergence of contemporary approaches and designs, offers endless possibilities—this can be both exhilarating and intimidating. Finding my personal aesthetic took some time.

A couple of years into my quilting career, I found myself a bit stuck. I'd experimented with both traditional designs and entirely improvisational approaches, but hadn't yet found a style that felt truly fresh and unique—that really came naturally. One evening, I decided to make the simplest striped quilt. I cut up dozens of solid-colored strips and pieced them together freely. No fuss. No stress. I was hooked. From then on, I began to focus on simplicity and basic geometric designs, on a combination of freewheeling techniques and measurement.

My hope is that the projects in this book will help fellow quilters, novice and seasoned, appreciate the liberty within a simplified approach to quiltmaking. Less really can be more. Each project should be treated like a coloring-book page on which the outlines are continuously shifting, offering a guideline within which you are free to explore your own use of color, dimension, and style. By focusing on the most basic geometric motifs—squares, circles, and stripes—the patterns in this book leave plenty of room for personal interpretation, resulting in unique, eye-catching, and elegant designs.

I've included basic quiltmaking instructions at the back of this book, beginning on page 71. However, this is not a book about making *perfect* quilts. I have tremendous respect for the precision and skilled technique inherent within the quilting tradition. However, I also believe in balancing this focus on craftsmanship with an attitude toward quiltmaking that is enjoyable, carefree, and relaxed. These are quilts to be loved and used, to cuddle under or wrap around your shoulders. These are items for brightening your day and adding color to your life. Precisely square corners and immaculately straight stitching lines aren't necessary.

While these projects are simple enough for the beginning sewist, experienced quilters will likely find a new realm of quilting possibilities here as well. The only requirement is that you enjoy yourself—loosen up and stitch with heart and soul.

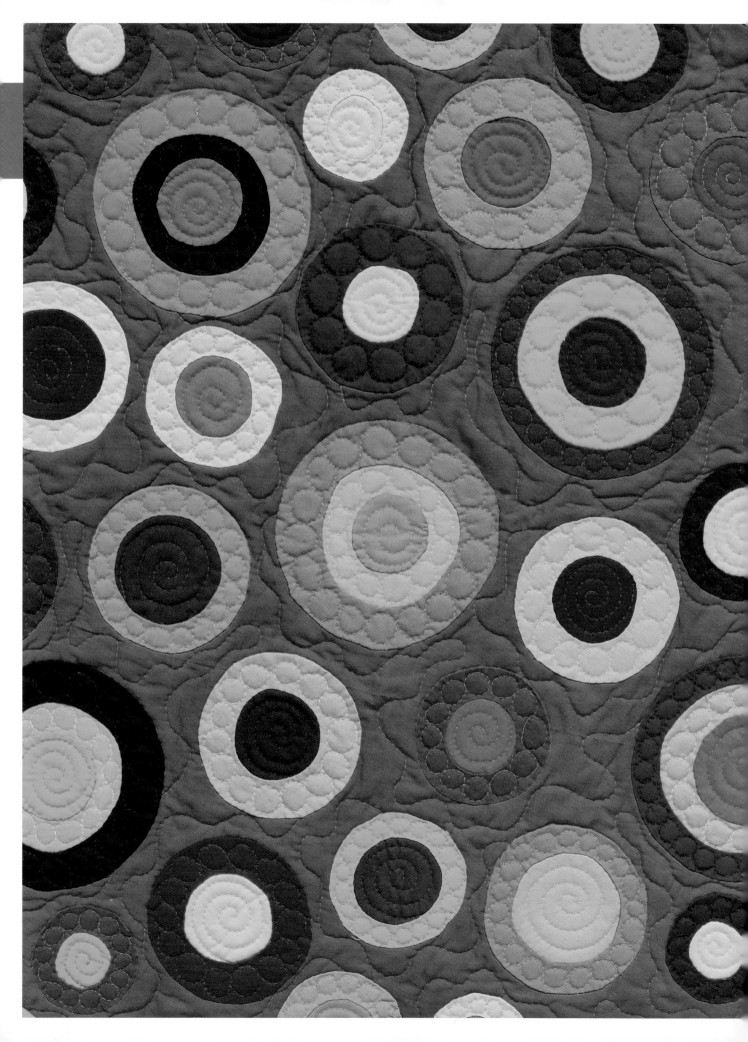

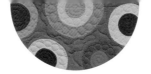

The Joy of Color

As my family, friends, and wardrobe will attest, I have an insatiable appetite for color. I just can't get enough—from cheery bright hues to rich earthy tones. I believe that all colors and all arrangements have their own beauty and particular strengths.

All the projects in this book use solid-colored fabrics. I like to think of quilt designs as blank canvases to be filled in with whatever bright, bold, and rich hues strike my fancy. Though I occasionally use patterned fabrics for backing smaller projects, I find that working exclusively with solids ensures that the finished project is fresh, simple, and striking.

We all have different visual preferences, and I don't follow any strict rules when selecting which colors I'm going to use in a quilt. However, a basic understanding of color principles can be a useful guide when it comes to selecting fabrics and arranging colors in your work.

BASIC TERMINOLOGY

The term *hue* refers to a color in its purest and brightest form. A *tint* is any hue with white added, and is also known as a pastel; tints create a softer, subtler color scheme. A *shade* is any hue with black added; shades create a darker, more dramatic effect. A *tone* has gray (both black and white) added.

A quilt design will take on a very different feel depending on how you choose to incorporate these elements of color. For instance, working with various tints, shades, and tones of a single hue creates one unique effect, while working with contrasting hues creates another.

THE COLOR WHEEL

The color wheel is an excellent starting point for thinking about how colors go together. You can use it as a guide when selecting and arranging colors, but by no means should you feel bound to its premises. Have fun experimenting with your own color combinations—remember that your personal visual preference is the most important thing.

Analogous colors are those that are next to each other on the color wheel, such as blue-violet, blue, and blue-green. They go together easily, creating a serene effect.

Complementary colors are opposite each other on the color wheel, such as red and green. The contrast between these colors creates a more energetic, intense appearance.

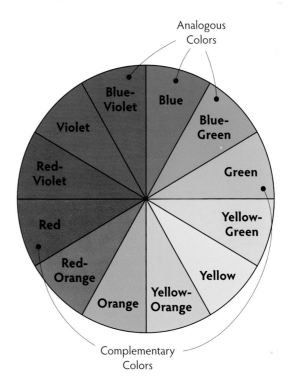

Nested Squares

FINISHED QUILT: 72½" x 96½"
FINISHED BLOCKS: 12" x 12"

"Nested" just seems like the best term for describing this design—the way the interior squares are enveloped in bands of a contrasting color. The quilt top is composed using basic piecing methods, but with an improvisational twist that makes every block and every finished quilt unique. By varying the width of the bands that surround each square, you'll add character and a slightly off-kilter look to an otherwise straightforward pattern. This method of freewheeling patchwork does result in some leftover fabrics, but a resourceful quilter always makes good use of extras!

MATERIALS

Yardage is based on 42"-wide fabric.

1¼ yards *each* of 10 different solid fabrics for blocks: red, purple, green, lime green, orange, yellow, aqua, dark blue, dark pink, and magenta in the quilt shown
⅝ yard of brown fabric for binding
6¼ yards of flannel for backing
81" x 105" piece of batting

CUTTING

From *each* of 8 solid fabrics, cut:
5 squares, 6½" x 6½"

From *each* of the 2 remaining solid fabrics, cut:
4 squares, 6½" x 6½"

From the remaining yardage of each fabric, cut:
42"-long strips ranging in width from 2½" to 5½" *

From the binding fabric, cut:
9 strips, 2" x 42"

*Aim for a variety of widths from each color, and use up all remaining fabric.

CREATING THE BLOCKS

1. Select one 6½" square. Sew a strip of a different color to one edge of the square, lining up the long edge of the strip with the side of the square. Trim off the excess fabric so the strip is even with the square; press the seam allowances open or away from the square.

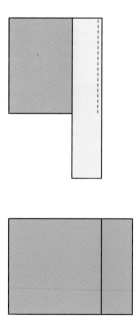

2. Repeat step 1 on the opposite side of the square with a strip of the same color; vary the width of the strip, but be sure that the finished width of the two strips and the square is at least 12½". (The width can be greater than 12½" since you will trim the block when done.)

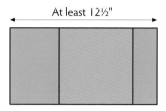

At least 12½"

3. Repeat steps 1 and 2 for the remaining sides of the unit, again ensuring a finished width of at least 12½".

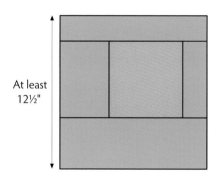

At least 12½"

4. Trim the block to 12½" x 12½". (You may want to wait to do this step until all the blocks have been sewn.)

5. Repeat steps 1–4 to make a total of 48 blocks. Aim for a roughly even amount of color distribution, using each color in four to five blocks.

·····Organize and Improvise·····

I like to work with one central-square color at a time, making all four or five blocks that have the same color in the center. I keep the strips in neat piles next to my sewing machine and select various widths as I go without too much planning or fuss. I prefer to have some blocks with the middle square nearly centered and other blocks that are very off-center, with strips as narrow as 2½" and as wide as 5½". Loosen up, improvise, and have fun!

ASSEMBLING THE QUILT TOP

1. Sew together six blocks to make a row, alternating the block orientation as shown. Press the seam allowances open. Make eight rows. Improvise the color arrangements, but keep an eye on the previous row to ensure that you have no two pieces of the same color next to each other in the final arrangement.

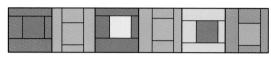

Make 8.

2. Align the seams between the blocks, and sew the rows together.

FINISHING

1. Cut the backing fabric in half so you have two pieces of fabric that are 42" x 108". Sew the two pieces together along their 108" lengths to form one large piece of backing, approximately 83½" x 108".

2. Baste your quilt and quilt as desired. I free-motion machine stitched a square spiral in each center square and a meandering design in the surrounding strips, matching the thread color to the fabric.

3. Stitch the binding strips into one continuous strip and bind your quilt.

Autumn Shades

The slightly muted tones in this variation give the quilt an autumnal feel—browns, deep green, gold, and plum create a more serene visual effect than the brighter tones in the main quilt shown. You can also use more than 10 colors in your quilt top, or fewer; you could limit your palette to a range within the same hue, or expand it to include even more contrasting colors.

Spots on Squares

FINISHED QUILT: 48½" x 60½"
FINISHED BLOCKS: 12" x 12"

This simple quilt combines just two basic shapes, yet it is still vivid and eye-catching. The circles seem to hover over the patchwork background, like lily pads floating on a pond. While the background consists of simple patchwork, the hand-appliquéd circles offer an opportunity to become immersed in the more meditative quality of hand stitching. You can replicate the colors in the quilt shown, but I encourage you to pick your own palette and have fun arranging the background squares and circles as you go, mixing up the colors so they contrast and complement.

MATERIALS

Yardage is based on 42"-wide fabric.

½ yard *each* of 10 different solid fabrics for background squares: brown, coral, dark purple, dark green, dark red, medium red, medium green, bright blue, dark blue, and burgundy in the quilt shown

¼ yard *each* of 12 different solid fabrics for appliqué circles: turquoise, amber, bright green, yellow, magenta, orange, green, medium blue, pink, dark pink, light blue, and maroon in the quilt shown

½ yard of green fabric for binding
4 yards of flannel for backing
57" x 69" piece of batting
Template plastic
Fabric pen or pencil

CUTTING

Make templates for the circle and half circle using the pattern on page 17. Trace the shapes onto selected fabrics; add a ¼" seam allowance outside of the marked line when cutting.

From *each* of the 10 background fabrics, cut:
2 squares, 12½" x 12½"

From *each* of 8 circle fabrics, cut:
3 circles

From *each* of the 4 remaining circle fabrics, cut:
2 circles

From *each* of 10 circle fabrics, cut:
1 half circle

From *each* of the 2 remaining circle fabrics, cut:
2 half circles

From the binding fabric, cut:
6 strips, 2" x 42"

CREATING THE QUILT TOP

1. Arrange the 12½" x 12½" squares in five rows of four squares each. You can plan ahead or arrange your colors at random; just keep in mind that you don't want two squares of the same color next to one another. Sew the blocks into rows and then sew the rows together.

Make 5.

2. Referring to "Hand Appliqué" on page 73, lay the pieced background on top of the batting if desired. Arrange the appliqué circles on top, placing one circle in the center of each square, and one at each intersection of four squares. Rearrange the colors until you are pleased with the placement. See "Easy Circle Placement" below for tips on positioning your circles.

····Easy Circle Placement····················

To find the center of the appliqué circles, fold them in half, and then in half again so you have a quarter circle; the folded point is the middle of the circle. Align this point with the intersection of four squares, or place it at the center of one of the squares (6" in from each side). Then carefully unfold the circle and pin. For the half circles, simply fold them in half once and align the fold with the seam of the two squares.

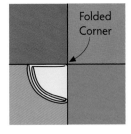

3. Pin each circle and half circle in place. Stitch each circle using hand appliqué. I find it easiest to work from the outside in (starting with the half circles)

so I'm not maneuvering in the center of lots of pins.

FINISHING

1. Cut the backing fabric in half so you have two pieces of fabric that are 42" x 72". Sew the two pieces together along their 72" lengths to form one large piece of backing fabric, approximately 72" x 83½". Trim to approximately 58" x 70".

2. Baste your quilt and quilt as desired. I free-motion machine stitched a spiral in the center of each circle, and outline stitched twice around the border of each square with stitching lines about ¾" apart using a matching thread color.

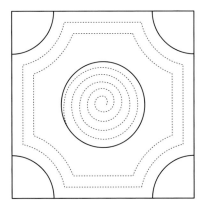

3. Stitch the binding strips into one continuous strip and bind your quilt.

Beige and Blue

The patchwork squares in this quilt are all shades of beige and brown, creating a backdrop that is subtler and more neutral than the featured project. Most of the circles are various shades of blue and green; limiting the palettes in this way creates a different kind of focus, exploring the nuances of fewer hues rather than the contrasts between many.

Pattern does not include seam allowance.

Half circle

Rotate and align pattern on dashed line to make full circle pattern.

Stacked Stripes

FINISHED QUILT: 65½" x 83"

Simple stripes are what first inspired my appreciation of minimalist geometric designs. They epitomize the quilt aesthetic that I'm most drawn to—both striking and understated, showcasing the selected colors as they mingle together on the quilt top. That being said, strips of fabric can be tricky to work with, so I try to embrace their tendency to curve and generally not cooperate. I even like the slightly slanted look you get from not cutting the edges of strip rows perfectly perpendicular. Those little quirks add character. You can choose fewer or more colors than the quilt shown, use each colored stripe an equal number of times or vary their frequency as I did—whatever best suits your style and your fabric stash.

MATERIALS

Yardage is based on 42"-wide fabric.

¼ to ½ yard *each* of 13 different solid fabrics for short stripes: plum, butterscotch, turquoise, medium purple, dark purple, red, lime green, medium blue, dark red, medium green, dark green, yellow, and dark pink in the quilt shown

1½ yards of dark-brown fabric for long stripes

⅞ yard of brick-red fabric for long stripes

⅝ yard of light-brown fabric for binding

5¼ yards of flannel for backing

74" x 91" piece of batting

CUTTING

From the 13 solid fabrics, cut *a total of:*
78 strips, 3" x 18" *

From the dark-brown fabric, cut:
16 strips, 3" x 42"

From the brick-red fabric, cut:
8 strips, 3" x 42"

From the binding fabric, cut:
8 strips, 2" x 42"

The number of strips cut from each color is up to you. In the quilt shown, the number from each color varies from 3 to 10.

Embrace Imprecision

Don't worry about measuring the 3" width of the 18"-long strips *too* precisely. If you cut some slightly narrower or wider, you'll create visual interest, and any extra fabric can be trimmed during the final assembly.

ASSEMBLING THE QUILT TOP

1. Sew together 26 of the 3" x 18" strips along their long edges until you have a total width of at least 65½". Make three of these stripe units. If necessary, trim the edges of the rows to even them out; it's OK if the final strips are less than 18".

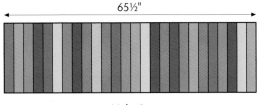

65½"

Make 3.

2. Sew together two of the dark-brown strips using a diagonal seam, as you would for binding strips. Trim the seam allowances to ¼" and press them open. Trim the strip to 65½" long. Make a total of eight strips.

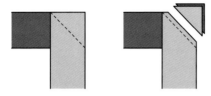

3. In the same manner, sew together the eight strips cut from brick-red fabric to create a total of four 65½"-long strips.

4. Sew a dark-brown 65½"-long strip to each side of a brick-red strip. Repeat to make four.

Make 4.

5. Sew the stripe units from step 1 together with the brown units from step 4 as shown.

FINISHING

1. Cut the backing fabric in half so you have two pieces of fabric that are 42" x 94". Sew the two pieces together along their 94" lengths to form one large piece of backing, approximately 83½" x 94". Trim to approximately 75" x 94".

2. Baste your quilt and quilt as desired. I free-motion machine stitched zigzags in each stripe, matching the thread color to the fabric.

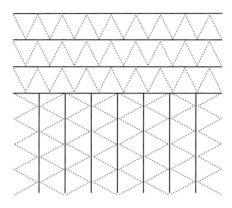

3. Stitch the binding strips into one continuous strip and bind your quilt.

•••• Ocean Waves ••••••••••••••••••••••••••

This version of the quilt uses only shades of blue for the vertical stripes, and red and purple for the horizontal bands. Focusing the color palette allows the monochromatic vertical segments to really contrast with the horizontal stripes for a more dramatic effect.

Twice Spliced

The random insertion of two-toned squares and stripes mixes up the colors and shapes in this otherwise straightforward quilt. Since square quilts don't really have a "correct" orientation, you have plenty of freedom to play around with the patchwork. You can plan out the arrangement of the two-tone elements or insert them at random, varying the pattern to make a quilt that is uniquely your own.

MATERIALS

Yardage is based on 42"-wide fabric.

1 yard of solid fabric for pieced squares and border stripes: medium purple in the quilt shown

⅞ yard *each* of 3 different solid fabrics for squares and pieced stripes: red, orange, and yellow in the quilt shown

¾ yard of solid fabric for pieced squares and border stripes: light blue in the quilt shown

⅝ yard *each* of 2 different solid fabrics for pieced squares and border stripes: bright blue and medium blue in the quilt shown

½ yard of solid fabric for pieced squares and border stripes: dark purple in the quilt shown

⅝ yard of bright-green fabric for binding

4½ yards of flannel for backing

75" x 75" piece of batting

What to Cut

If you don't follow the pattern precisely, instead coming up with your own color combinations and placements for the spliced shapes, you may need a different number of shapes than those listed. You can plan ahead and cut exactly the right amount, or cut the necessary pieces as you go, depending on your preferred style of working.

CUTTING

From the first solid for squares and pieced stripes (red), cut:
18 squares, 6½" x 6½"
2 strips, 2½" x 42"

From *each* of the second and third solids for squares and pieced stripes (orange and yellow), cut:
17 squares, 6½" x 6½"
2 strips, 2½" x 42"

From the first solid for pieced squares and border stripes (bright blue), cut:
4 squares, 6½" x 6½"
14 strips, 2½" x 12½"

From the second solid for pieced squares and border stripes (medium purple), cut:
7 squares, 6½" x 6½"
17 strips, 2½" x 12½"

From the third solid for pieced squares and border stripes (medium blue), cut:
5 squares, 6½" x 6½"
15 strips, 2½" x 12½"

From the fourth solid for pieced squares and border stripes (light blue), cut:
5 squares, 6½" x 6½"
16 strips, 2½" x 12½"

Continued on page 23

From the fifth solid for pieced squares and border stripes (dark purple), cut:
5 squares, 6½" x 6½"
8 strips, 2½" x 12½"

From the binding fabric, cut:
7 strips, 2" x 42"

MAKING THE PIECED SQUARES

1. Select two contrasting 6½" squares cut from the solids for pieced squares (purples and blues). Fold one of the squares in half along the diagonal and press. (You can draw a diagonal line from corner to corner if you prefer.)

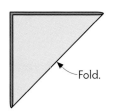

Fold.

2. Open the pressed or marked square and place it on top of the other square, right sides facing. Sew along the pressed or drawn line. Trim ¼" from the sewn line and press the seam allowances open.

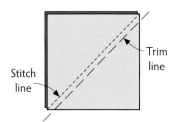

Trim line

Stitch line

3. Repeat steps 1 and 2 to create 12 additional pieced squares.

MAKING THE PIECED STRIPES

1. Using a diagonal seam, sew together two contrasting 2½" x 42" strips cut from the solids for pieced stripes. Trim ¼" from the sewn line, and press the seam allowances open.

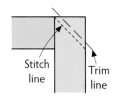

Stitch line

Trim line

2. Trim each end of the long strip so that the center portion measures 12½". Don't worry about getting the diagonal seam centered exactly in the middle of the strip.

3. Using the remaining strips, repeat steps 1 and 2 to create a total of 14 pieced stripes.

···· **Changing Directions** ·······················

When making the pieced stripes, alternate the angle of the diagonal seam; this is done by changing the direction in which you lay the second strip perpendicular to the first before sewing.

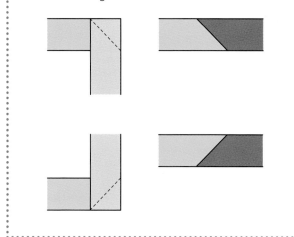

ASSEMBLING THE QUILT TOP

You can insert the pieced squares and stripes according to the diagram, or wherever you choose. Feel free to play around and improvise. However, notice that the solid stripes and squares fall in sequential color order (red, orange, yellow, red, orange, yellow, etc.). Whenever you insert a pieced shape, consider this a substitute in the sequence (red, orange, pieced, red, orange, yellow, etc.).

1. Sew seven 6½" squares together to make a row, inserting one or two pieced squares as desired. Make seven rows.

Make 7.

2. Lining up the seams between the blocks, sew the rows together.

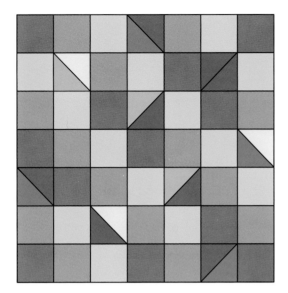

3. Make a corner block by sewing together two rows of two blocks each, including one pieced square in one of the rows. Sew the rows together to create a Four Patch block. Make four blocks.

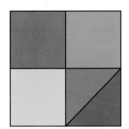

Make 4.

4. Sew 21 of the 2½" x 12½" strips together, inserting the pieced stripes as shown, or as you choose. Make four border units.

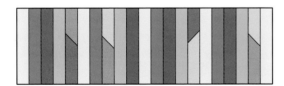

Make 4.

5. Sew border units to opposite sides of the quilt center, lining up the seams so that there are three strips for each square.

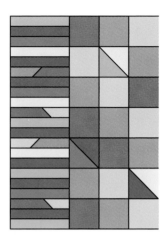

6. Sew a corner Four Patch block to each short end of the remaining border units.

7. Sew the border units created in step 6 to the remaining edges of the quilt.

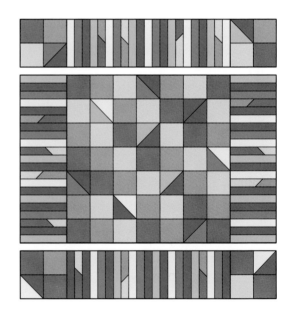

twice spliced

FINISHING

1. Cut the backing fabric in half so you have two pieces of fabric that are 42" x 81". Sew the two pieces together along their 81" lengths to form one large piece of backing, approximately 81" x 83½". Trim to approximately 76" square.

2. Baste your quilt and quilt as desired. I free-motion machine stitched diagonal lines within the squares and zigzags within each stripe, matching the thread color to the fabric.

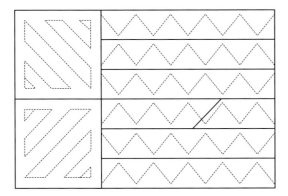

3. Stitch the binding strips into one continuous strip and bind your quilt.

Midnight Lights

Combining neutral black, gray, and navy tones with brighter hues makes the contrast between the solid and spliced shapes even more prominent. The quilting pattern in this version is also different, with a staircase design stitched over the central squares, and zigzags stitched vertically rather than horizontally along the strip areas. I used fewer pieced squares in this version, leaving them out of two of the corner blocks. Include as many or as few as you like in your own quilt.

Rainbow Road

FINISHED QUILT: 51½" x 54½"

This unfussy geometric design contrasts a sparkling strip of patchwork against a large area of neutral solid fabric. The distinct difference between the two areas emphasizes the rich pattern of little squares and expanses of a single color. This is an ideal stash-busting project, and can be stitched up in a day. You'll really have fun with color when making the patchwork band—use your scraps or whatever you have on hand and don't plan the arrangements beforehand. You could use any solid color for the background, but I find that a neutral hue best complements the multicolored patchwork.

MATERIALS

Yardage is based on 42"-wide fabric.

1¾ yards of dark-gray solid or other neutral fabric for background

¾ yard *total* of at least 10 different solid fabrics for patchwork band

½ yard of coral-pink fabric for binding

3½ yards of flannel for backing

60" x 63" piece of batting

CUTTING

From the 10 different solid fabrics, cut *a total of:*
135 squares, 2½" x 2½"

From the dark-gray background fabric, cut:*
1 rectangle, 12" x 54½"
1 rectangle, 30" x 54½"

From the binding fabric, cut:
6 strips, 2" x 42"

*It's OK if your fabric isn't quite 42" wide; simply cut the two rectangles a bit narrower.

ASSEMBLING THE QUILT TOP

1. Sew five 2½" squares together to make a row.

2. Repeat step 1 to create a second row of five squares; sew this to the first row, lining up the seams between the squares.

3. Continue sewing rows of five squares, adding each one to the previously sewn rows as you go. (This makes it easier to keep track of the color placement and avoids having two squares of the same color next to each other.) Repeat until you have a total of 27 rows sewn together.

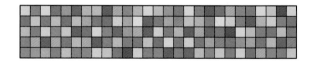

4. Sew the gray 12" x 54½" rectangle to the patch-work band along the long edges. Sew the gray 30" x 54½" rectangle to the opposite side of the patchwork band to finish the quilt top.

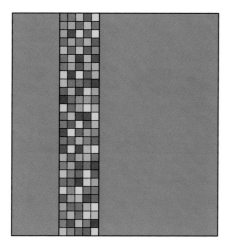

FINISHING

1. Cut the backing fabric in half so you have two pieces of fabric that are 42" x 63". Sew the two pieces together along their 63" lengths to form one large piece of backing, approximately 63" x 83½". Trim to approximately 63" x 65".

2. Baste your quilt and quilt as desired. I free-motion machine stitched a stippling pattern over the patchwork band using beige thread. In the back-ground I stitched straight, machine-guided vertical lines a little less than 1" apart using gray thread to match the neutral background.

3. Stitch the binding strips into one continuous strip and bind your quilt.

This variation still uses up plenty of fabric scraps, but only those that are tints and shades of blue. I also reversed the quilting motifs, so the stippling is on the background and the vertical lines are on the patchwork band. Changing the textures of the two areas gives the quilt an entirely different feel; the back-ground becomes soft and swirly, while the patchwork band becomes more geometric.

Scattering Squares

It's amazing how size variations and repetition of one basic shape can achieve such a distinctive and modern design. The three sizes of squares and the kinetic scattering pattern of this quilt remind me of a sidewalk or brick grid. You can use up some scraps for the smaller squares, and include as many colors as you like. This is also a great beginner's project since it involves easy cutting and straightforward piecing techniques.

MATERIALS

Yardage is based on 42"-wide fabric.

½ yard *each* of 10 different solid fabrics for large, medium, and small squares
¼ yard *each* of 5 different solid fabrics for remaining medium and small squares
½ yard of blue fabric for binding
3¼ yards of flannel for backing
57" x 69" piece of batting

CUTTING

From *each* of the 10 fabrics for large squares, cut:
1 square, 12½" x 12½"

From the combined 15 fabrics for squares, cut *a total of:*
25 squares, 6½" x 6½"
60 squares, 3½" x 3½"

From the binding fabric, cut:
6 strips, 2" x 42"

ASSEMBLING THE QUILT TOP

To make construction of the quilt top easier, it's assembled in sections, which are then joined to form the entire quilt top. Refer to the assembly diagram on page 31 as you sew one section at a time. Arrange the colors randomly, but avoid placing two squares of an identical color next to one another.

1. **Section 1:** Sew together eight 3½" squares in a row. Make four rows. Sew the rows together to create a rectangle.

2. **Section 2:** Sew two rows of two 3½" squares each. Sew the rows together to create a four-patch unit. Sew this unit to a 6½" square.

3. **Section 3:** Sew two rows of three 3½" squares each. Sew the rows together to create a rectangle.

4. **Section 4:** Sew four rows of four 3½" squares each. Sew the rows together.

5. **Sections 5 and 8:** Repeat step 2 to make these sections.

6. **Sections 6 and 9:** Repeat step 3 to make these sections.

7. **Sections 10, 12, and 13:** Sew two 12½" squares together to make section 10, sew three 12½" squares together to make section 12, and sew four 12½" squares together to make section 13.

8. Sew the sections and one additional 12½" square (section 7) together into five rows as shown in the diagram. Sew the rows together to complete the quilt top.

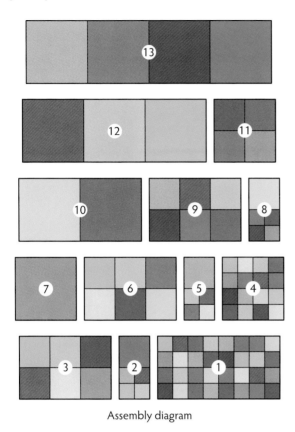

Assembly diagram

FINISHING

1. Cut the backing fabric in half so you have two pieces of fabric that are 42" x 58". Sew the two pieces together along their 58" lengths to form one large piece of backing, approximately 58" x 83½". Trim to approximately 58" x 70".

2. Baste your quilt and quilt as desired. I free-motion machine stitched one large spiral design in beige thread over the entire quilt top, beginning at the center of the quilt.

3. Stitch the binding strips into one continuous strip and bind your quilt.

···Grass Green··································

Using only shades of green gives the quilt top a more blended appearance, subduing the "scattering" effect in favor of a cohesive look. In addition, the meandering quilting stitches create a bumpier texture; combined with the green palette, this enhances the grass-like appearance of the quilt.

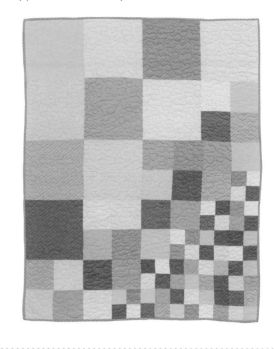

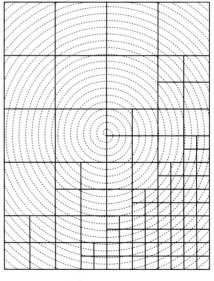

Quilting suggestion

Bouncing Beach Balls

There's something so whimsical and lively about the image of beach balls bouncing in the air. I also love the colors of the beach—not just the blue ocean and yellow sand, but the vibrant array of towels, umbrellas, and toys. What better theme for a baby quilt? Have fun rearranging the beach balls as you choose, and if you want to use up your scraps, you can always include more than two colors in each ball.

MATERIALS

Yardage is based on 42"-wide fabric.

⅞ yard of solid fabric for background: red in the quilt shown

¼ yard *each* of 2 different solid fabrics for large beach balls: yellow and aqua in the quilt shown

¼ yard *each* of 2 different solid fabrics for small beach balls: lime green and purple in the quilt shown

⅓ yard of aqua fabric for binding

1⅜ yards of flannel for backing

34" x 44" piece of batting

Template plastic

Fabric pen or pencil

CUTTING

Make templates for the beach balls using the large and small patterns on page 35. Trace the wedges onto selected fabrics.

From the background fabric, cut:
1 rectangle, 26" x 36"

From *each* of the fabrics for large beach balls, cut:
6 large beach-ball wedges

From *each* of the fabrics for small beach balls, cut:
9 small beach-ball wedges

From the binding fabric, cut:
4 strips, 2" x 42"

CREATING THE BEACH BALLS

1. Sew two different-colored large wedges together; start stitching ¼" from the narrow point of the wedges, and stitch all the way to the curved edge. Press the seam allowances open.

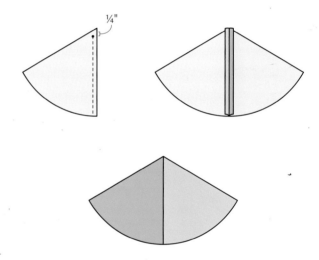

2. Sew another large wedge to this unit in a similar manner, alternating the colors, to create a half circle.

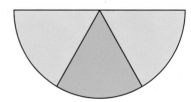

3. Repeat steps 1 and 2 to create a second half circle, arranging the colors in opposite positions from the first half.

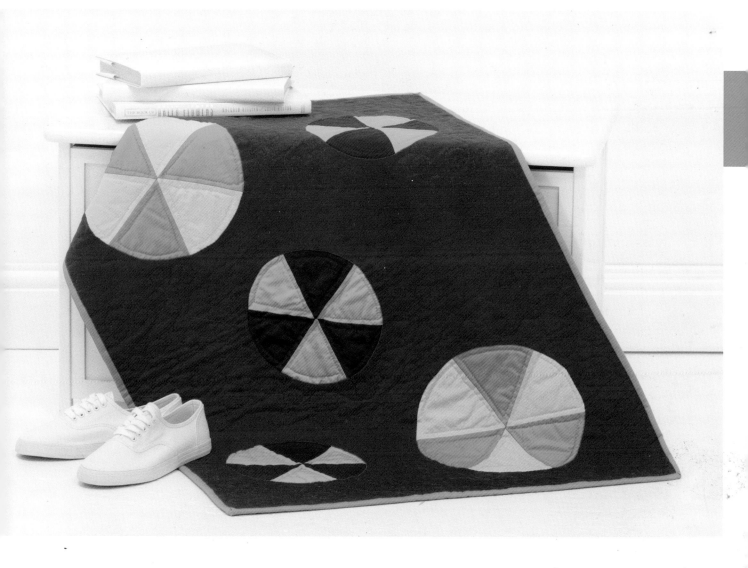

4. Sew the two halves together along the long edge to create a complete beach ball, lining up the central points between the three wedges. Trim the seam allowances at the center to reduce bulk.

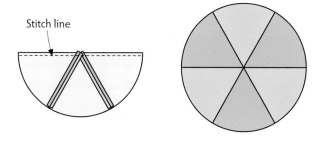

Stitch line

5. Repeat steps 1–4 to create a second large beach ball and three small beach balls.

APPLIQUÉING THE BEACH BALLS

The beach balls are added to the quilt top using reverse appliqué; I find that it's easier to turn under the background fabric than to turn under the pieced ball with seam allowances, and I like the more embedded appearance this gives the beach balls. Refer to "Reverse Appliqué" on page 75 for additional details.

1. Make two circle templates, one with a 9½" diameter and the other with an 8" diameter. You can use a compass, or mark a center point and draw approximately 20 lines the length of the diameter (either 4" or 4¾") out from the central line, then connect the ends of these lines with a curving circumference. Cut out your templates.

2. Using the templates, draw two large beach balls and three small beach balls on what will be the wrong side of your background fabric. Use the quilt layout diagram on page 34 as a general guide for placement, but don't worry about measuring precisely—you can choose an entirely different arrangement if you like.

3. Prepare the background fabric for reverse appliqué: cut inside the drawn circle lines, leaving a ¼"

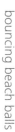

bouncing beach balls

seam allowance, and then cut slits every ¼"
almost to the drawn line. Lay the background
fabric on the batting if desired, and smooth or
iron it out. Insert the patchwork beach balls into
the center of each open space, tucking the edges
underneath the background fabric. Pin the beach
balls in place on the batting and pin through the
background fabric and batting around the perimeter of each ball.

4. Turn under the seam allowance on the marked line
and appliqué each ball in place.

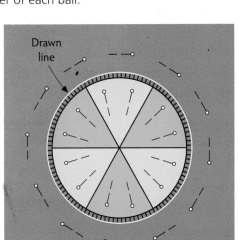

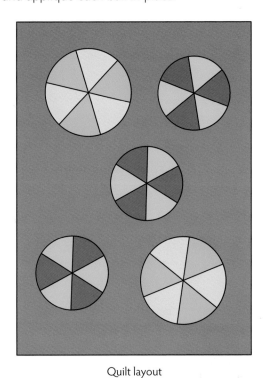

Quilt layout

Large beach ball

FINISHING

1. Baste your quilt and quilt as desired. I stitched swirls and loops in the background to create the suggestion of blowing wind, and stitched about ¼" from the seams within each beach-ball wedge to echo the geometry of the balls, matching the thread color to the fabric.

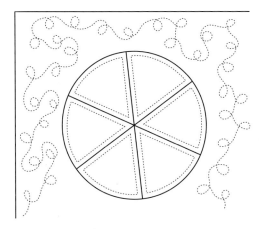

2. Stitch the binding strips into one continuous strip and bind your quilt.

Small beach ball

The use of a more muted palette and multiple colors within each beach ball evokes the feeling of a playground in autumn more than a summer beach party. The circular quilting echoes the shapes of the balls so they appear to be floating on the background, rather than bouncing in the air.

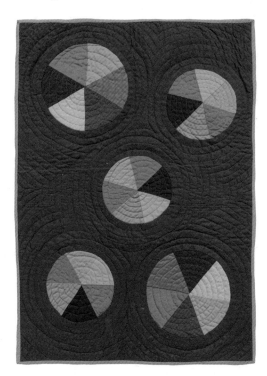

Diced Diagonals Throw Pillow

FINISHED PILLOW: 20" x 20"

Slanted stripes converge into a diamond shape in this singular but straightforward design. The pillow top consists of four blocks that are improvisationally pieced together, and then trimmed to the same size. You'll get used to the freewheeling approach to piecing strips after the first block. Experimenting with different color arrangements can dramatically alter the feel of this piece, so don't hesitate to try out a variety of combinations.

MATERIALS

Yardage is based on 42"-wide fabric.

¼ yard *each* of 8 different solid fabrics for pillow front: magenta, lime green, yellow, brown, red, dark purple, aqua, and orange in the pillow shown

¾ yard of flannel for pillow back

24" x 24" piece of muslin

24" x 24" piece of batting

20" x 20" pillow form

CUTTING

From *each* of the 8 solid fabrics, cut:
2 strips, approximately 2" x 42" *

From the flannel, cut:
2 pieces, approximately 20" x 27"

Given the nature of this piecing method, the strips don't need to be exactly 2" wide. Feel free to eyeball the width or experiment with a range of widths.

IMPROVISATIONAL PIECING

To create each block, you'll sew strips together and then cut a 10½" square from the pieced fabric. A large 12½" square ruler is very helpful to make sure your strips are long enough. Trim the 2" x 42" strips as you go and hold the block up to the ruler periodically, ensuring that it is at least 10½" square with the strips running at a 45° angle. The strip lengths given in the steps are just a guide; you may find you need shorter or longer strips as you work. Press the seam allowances open or in one direction after adding each strip.

1. Sew together a 2" x 4" strip and a contrasting 2" x 7" strip, centering the 4" strip along the longer strip.

2. Alternating the same two colors, sew an 11" strip to the 7" strip, centering the shorter strip on the longer strip. Then sew a 13" strip to the 11" strip, and a 16" strip to the 13" strip.

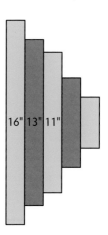

3. Continue adding strips in this manner, sewing a second 16" strip to the first and then adding shorter strip lengths. Sew a 13" strip to the 16" strip, an 11" strip to the 13" strip, a 7" strip to the 11" strip, and a 4" strip to the 7" strip.

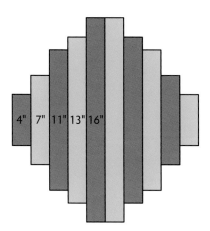

4. Hold the resulting block up to your ruler (or measure it on your rotary-cutting mat) with the strips at a 45° angle, and check that you can cut a 10½" square from the block; you may need to add another short strip at either end. Trim the block to 10½" x 10½" with the strips running at a 45° angle.

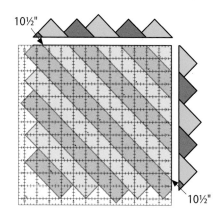

5. Repeat steps 1–4 to create three more blocks, using the remaining six colors and alternating two colors per block.

6. Sew two blocks together as shown, with the strips forming an inverted V. Repeat with the other two blocks, and then sew the rows of two blocks together, lining up the seams so the strips converge to form a diamond pattern.

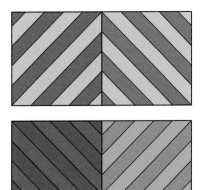

FINISHING

1. Baste the pillow top, batting, and muslin. Quilt as desired. I free-motion machine stitched narrow zig-zags along each strip, matching the thread color to the fabric.

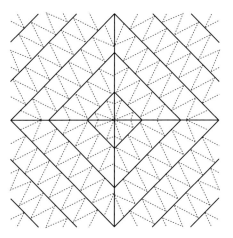

2. Trim the excess batting and muslin.

3. Fold under ½" along the 27"-long side of one of the flannel backing pieces and press. Fold another ½" and press again. Topstitch the hem with matching thread. Repeat with the second piece of backing fabric.

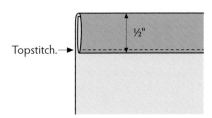

Topstitch. →   ½"

4. Layer the two pieces of backing fabric, right sides up, so they overlap about 3" along the folded edges.

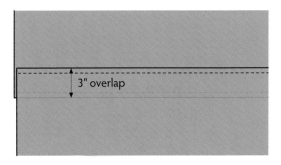

3" overlap

5. Center the pillow top, wrong side up, on top of the backing fabric, with the overlap running along the middle of the pillow top. Pin together the pillow top and backing, being sure to pin through all layers at the overlapping areas. There will be extra backing fabric around the edges; you will trim this after stitching.

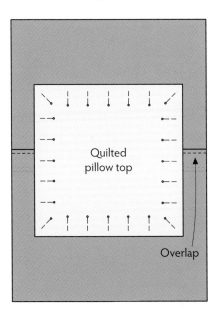

6. Sew around the perimeter of the pillow cover using a ¼" seam allowance. Trim the excess backing fabric and trim across the corners to reduce bulk. Zigzag stitch around the perimeter, catching the raw edges.

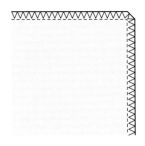

7. Turn the pillow cover right side out through the opening and push out the corners with a blunt-tipped object. Insert the pillow form.

In the Mix

By including a variety of strip colors that are randomly assorted, the design's focus becomes the overall diamond pattern, rather than the individual blocks. Quilting one continuous spiral enhances this effect, pulling the entire pillow top together. You could also use the same two colors for all the blocks, or use four different colors for two sets of matching blocks.

Half-and-Half Throw Pillow

FINISHED PILLOW: 18" x 18"

This project is the perfect way to add a little character and quirkiness to your living room, family room, or even bedroom. The opposition between two distinct shapes makes for a playful and unexpected design. I like how the pillow top almost looks like it's been spliced in half—yet another example of how unusual combinations of simple shapes can still be eye-catching and unique.

MATERIALS

Yardage is based on 42"-wide fabric.

¼ yard *each* of 2 different solid fabrics for squares: aqua and lime green in the pillow shown
¼ yard *each* of 2 different solid fabrics for stripes: magenta and orange in the pillow shown
¾ yard of flannel for pillow back
22" x 22" piece of muslin
22" x 22" piece of batting
18" x 18" pillow form

CUTTING

From the first fabric for squares, cut:
12 squares, 3½" x 3½"

From the second fabric for squares, cut:
9 squares, 3½" x 3½"

From *each* of the fabrics for stripes, cut:
1 strip, 2" x 14"
1 strip, 2" x 13"
1 strip, 2" x 11"
1 strip, 2" x 10"
1 strip, 2" x 8"
1 strip, 2" x 7"
1 strip, 2" x 5"
1 strip, 2" x 4"
1 strip, 2" x 3"

From the flannel, cut:
2 pieces, approximately 20" x 27"

ASSEMBLING THE PILLOW TOP

1. Sew the 3½" squares together in six rows as shown, alternating the colors.

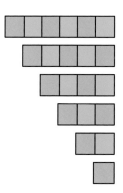

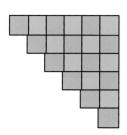

2. Trim along the diagonal of the unit, leaving ¼"
beyond the corners of the squares.

3. Sew the 2" strips together, alternating colors and
aligning them on one end as shown.

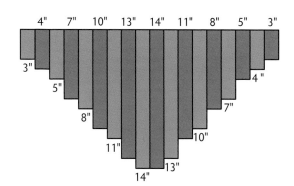

4. Sew the two pillow halves together, lining up the seam between the 14"-long strips with the seam between the two center squares along the diagonal. Before pressing the seam allowances open, trim the half made up of strips by cutting along the edge of the half made up of squares as shown. A large square ruler works well for this. Then press the seam allowances open.

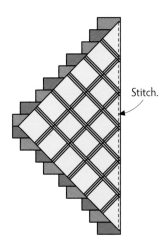

Stitch.

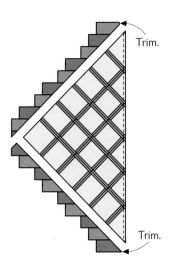

Trim.

Trim.

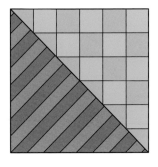

FINISHING

1. Baste the pillow top, batting, and muslin. Quilt as desired. I free-motion machine stitched square spirals within each of the squares, and a geometric pattern in the stripes, matching the thread color to the fabric.

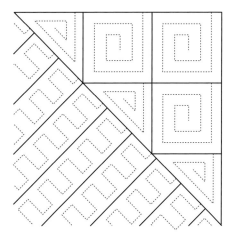

2. Refer to "Finishing" on page 38 and follow steps 2–7 to complete the pillow.

Grape and Green

In this version of the pillow, instead of using two colors for the squares and two for the stripes, I upped it to three, and kept all of them in the same hue range. The contrast between the two halves is still prominent, but each half is a little more dynamic on its own.

Fruity Rings Pillowcase

FINISHED PILLOWCASE: 20" x 29"

I'm always on the lookout for quilting inspiration, and it often pops up in the most unexpected places—for instance, in a breakfast bowl. Cereal is my husband's go-to breakfast, and I was immediately inspired when he brought home a box of Kellogg's Froot Loops. Colorful, geometric, simple—they're my dream quilt motif.

MATERIALS FOR 1 PILLOWCASE

Yardage is based on 42"-wide fabric.

⅔ yard of solid fabric for pillowcase background: red and purple in the projects shown

1 square, 5" x 5", *each* of 9 different solid fabrics for fruit loops

¾ yard of solid fabric for pillowcase back*

24" x 35" piece of muslin

24" x 35" piece of batting

Template plastic

Fabric pen or pencil

Standard-size bed pillow (20" x 26")

*Match the back fabric to the background for the pillowcase top, or use a contrasting color as I did.

CUTTING

Make a template of the fruity ring using the pattern on page 47. Trace the shape onto selected fabrics; add a ¼" seam allowance outside the marked line when cutting.

From the background fabric, cut:
1 rectangle, 20½" x 31½"

From *each* of the 9 solid squares, cut:
1 fruity ring

From the back fabric, cut:
1 rectangle, 24" x 33"

APPLIQUÉING THE PILLOWCASE TOP

1. Make a template of the ring center and trace it in the center of each loop. Cut out ¼" inside the drawn line, and clip into the seam allowance every ¼" almost to the drawn line.

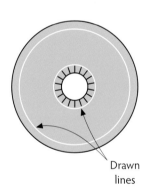

Drawn
lines

2. Referring to "Hand Appliqué" on page 73, lay the background fabric on top of the batting, if desired, right side up. Iron or smooth out the fabric. Arrange the rings as you like, trying to space them somewhat evenly. Leave about 5" of space at one of the short ends to allow for the pillow opening. Make sure that the rings and background fabric are lying flat and smooth. Pin all the rings in place, through the batting if you are using it.

3. Stitch each ring in place, appliquéing the inner circle first, and then the outer edge of the ring.

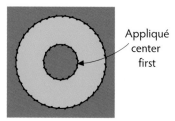

Appliqué center first

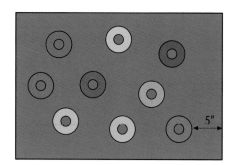

5"

FINISHING

1. Baste the pillowcase top, batting, and muslin. Use pins to mark a line 2" from and parallel to the pillow opening (the short side where you allowed extra space when arranging the rings).

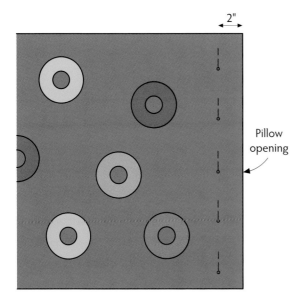

2. Quilt as desired, leaving the area beyond the pinned line unquilted. I free-motion machine quilted circles on the rings, and quilted meandering lines in the background, matching the thread colors to the fabric.

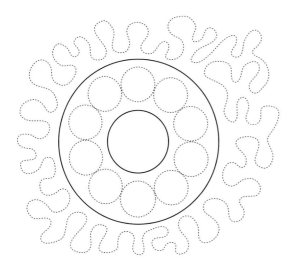

3. Remove all pins and trim the excess batting and muslin even with the pillowcase top. Fold back the unquilted area of the top and trim 1" from the underlying muslin and batting.

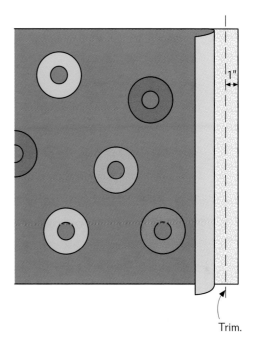

Trim.

4. Fold in 1" along the pillowcase top's short unquilted edge, and press. Fold in another 1" so the top wraps around the batting and muslin; press again. Topstitch along the edge of the fold with matching thread.

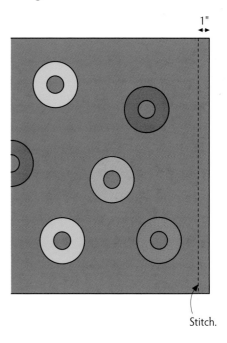

Stitch.

5. Using the 24" x 33" piece of pillowcase back fabric, fold in 1" along one short edge and press. Fold another 1", press again, and topstitch along the fold with matching thread.

6. Lay the pillowcase top on the pillowcase back fabric, right sides together. Line up the folded and stitched edges; there will be excess back fabric along the other three sides. Pin around the perimeter.

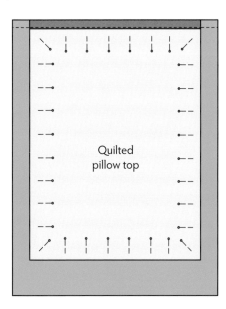

Quilted pillow top

7. Stitch around the perimeter using a ¼" seam allowance. Do not stitch the folded short ends; this is the pillowcase opening. Trim the excess back fabric and trim across the corners. Zigzag stitch around the perimeter, catching the raw edges.

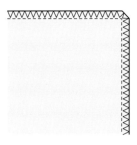

8. Turn the pillowcase right side out and push out the corners with a blunt-tipped object. Insert the pillow.

A brown background emphasizes the bright colors of the fruity rings. You could also experiment with using two each of three different-colored rings, or make all of the rings in different shades of the same hue.

Fruity ring

**Fruity ring
center**

Patterns do not include
seam allowances.

Dots and Dashes Lounge Pillow

FINISHED PILLOW: 20" x 36"

This extra-long pillow can be used on a bed or sofa; the term "lounge" just seems to capture the luxuriousness of its large size, perfect for snuggling up with while napping or unwinding with a good book. Naturally, it makes use of my three favorite shapes and in a fuss-free but fun arrangement. This is a good beginner's project since it combines basic patchwork and just a sampling of appliqué.

MATERIALS

Yardage is based on 42"-wide fabric.

⅓ yard *each* of 6 different solid fabrics for pillow top: red, blue, green, purple, pink, and yellow in the pillow shown
1½ yards of flannel for pillow back
24" x 40" piece of muslin
24" x 40" piece of batting
Template plastic
Fabric pen or pencil
King-size pillow form, 20" x 36"

Note: Label your colors 1 through 6. In the pillow shown, red is color 1, blue is 2, green is 3, purple is 4, pink is 5, and yellow is 6.

CUTTING

Make a template using the dot pattern on page 51. Trace the dot onto selected fabrics; add a ¼" seam allowance outside of the marked line when cutting.

From *each* of fabrics 1 and 2, cut:
2 strips, 2½" x 20½"
1 strip, 2½" x 9"
1 strip, 2½" x 8"

From *each* of fabrics 3 and 4, cut:
4 strips, 2½" x 12"
1 strip, 2½" x 4½"
1 strip, 2½" x 4"

From *each* of fabrics 5 and 6, cut:
2 strips, 2½" x 20½"
1 strip, 2½" x 7"
1 strip, 2½" x 10"

From *each* of fabrics 2, 3, and 6, cut:
1 square, 4½" x 4½"

From each of fabrics 1, 4, and 5, cut:
1 dot

From the flannel, cut:
2 pieces, 25" x 30"

MAKING BLOCK 1

1. Sew two of the 20½"-long strips cut from fabrics 1 and 2 together along their long edges. Make two of these units. Sew the two 2½" x 8" strips together along their long edges; repeat with the 2½" x 9" strips. Sew the 4½" square cut from fabric 3 between the short edges of the 8"- and 9"-long units as shown.

Make 2.

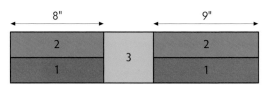

Make 1.

2. Sew the three units together along their long edges as shown, placing the 9"-long strips of the center unit at the bottom.

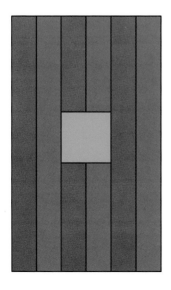

MAKING BLOCK 2

1. Sew four of the 2½" x 12" strips cut from fabrics 3 and 4 together along their long edges, alternating colors. Make two of these units. Sew the two 2½" x 4½" strips together along their long edges; repeat with the 2½" x 4" strips. Sew the 4½" square cut from fabric 6 between the short edges of the 4"- and 4½"-long units.

3
4
3
4

Make 2.

4"   4½"

3	6	3
4		4

Make 1.

2. Sew the three units together along their long edges as shown, with the unit containing the square in the middle, and the 4½" strips on the left.

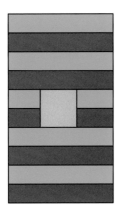

MAKING BLOCK 3

1. Sew two of the 2½" x 20½" strips cut from fabrics 5 and 6 together along their long edges. Make two of these units. Sew the two 2½" x 7" strips together along their long edges; repeat with the two 2½" x 10" strips. Sew the square cut from fabric 2 between the short edges of the 7"- and 10"-long units.

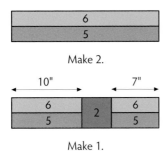

Make 2.

Make 1.

2. Sew the three units together along their long edges as shown, placing the 7" strips of the center unit at the bottom.

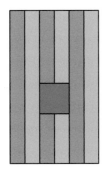

PILLOW ASSEMBLY AND APPLIQUÉ

1. Sew the three blocks together as shown, sewing block 2 to block 1, and block 3 to block 2, so that the stripes in block 2 run perpendicular to the stripes in blocks 1 and 3.

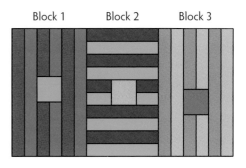

2. Referring to "Hand Appliqué" on page 73, center the dots in each of the three squares, arranging the colors as follows: fabric 4 circle in fabric 3 square, fabric 5 circle in fabric 6 square, and fabric 1 circle in fabric 2 square. Pin the circles to the background squares.

3. Hand appliqué the circles in place.

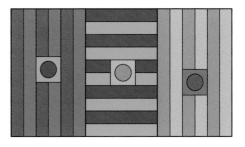

FINISHING

1. Baste the pillow top, batting, and muslin. Quilt as desired. I free-motion machine quilted a spiral in each circle, an undulating line in the surrounding square, and a geometric design in the strips using thread color that matched the fabrics. See the quilting diagram on the facing page.

2. Refer to "Finishing" on page 38 and follow steps 2–7 to complete the pillow. Use the 25" x 30" pieces of flannel and hem the 25" sides as directed.

Brightened Up a Notch

Brighter hues make for a more vibrant, summery pillow. You could also try using only four colors, or even more than six. I also used different quilting motifs in this version; the circular pattern in the strips generates a softer, bubbly texture.

Quilting idea

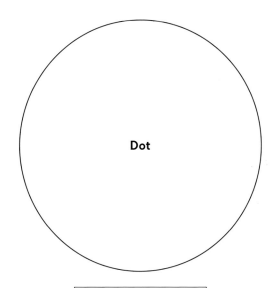

Dot

Pattern does not include seam allowance.

Spirals and Spots Table Runner

FINISHED TABLE RUNNER: 15" x 30½"

Table runners are such an easy way to add a little pizzazz to your dining-room space. I love decorating mine with matching decor that emphasizes the table setting or the season—everything from flower vases to pumpkins and candles. The design of this runner is easily adaptable to any dishware or time of year, so enjoy playing around with different colors.

MATERIALS

Yardage is based on 42"-wide fabric.

½ yard *each* of 2 different solid fabrics for spots and spot backgrounds: brown and orange in the table runner shown

⅓ yard *each* of 2 different solid fabrics for pieced rectangles: light blue and dark blue in the table runner shown

¼ yard of orange fabric for binding

⅝ yard of solid fabric for backing

19" x 35" piece of batting

Template plastic

Fabric pen or pencil

CUTTING

From *each* of the fabrics for pieced rectangles, cut:
4 strips, 2" x 42"; crosscut into:*
    9 strips, 2" x 10"
    3 strips, 2" x 6"
    3 strips, 2" x 4"

From the background fabric, cut:
3 rectangles, 5½" x 15"

*These lengths are minimums, but they don't have to be exact.

From the fabric for spots, cut:
3 rectangles, 5" x 14½"

From the binding fabric, cut:
3 strips, 2" x 42"

MAKING THE PIECED RECTANGLES

You will sew the rectangles together improvisationally, with strips of various lengths staggered at an angle. I find it helpful to keep a large rotary-cutting ruler nearby to ensure that I can cut a rectangle that is 5½" x 15" from this striped unit. I also cut the 42"-long strips into shorter strips as I go, eyeballing the correct length rather than precisely measuring and cutting beforehand, but you might find it helpful to have them precut.

1. Sew a 2" x 4" strip and a contrasting 2" x 6" strip together, roughly centering the 4" strip in the middle of the 6" strip.

2. Using the alternate color, sew an approximately 2" x 10" strip to the 6" strip, again roughly centering the 6" strip in the middle of the 10" strip. Sew a second 2" x 10" strip of the alternate color, staggering the strip so it is roughly 1" from the edge of the first. Continue adding 10" strips in this manner until you have six 10" strips. The unit should measure at least 15" along the left side. If it doesn't, add another 2" x 10" strip.

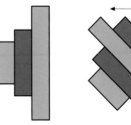
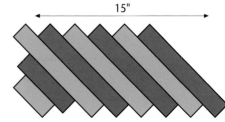

15"

3. Add another 2" x 6" strip and a 2" x 4" strip, centering the strips as you did at the beginning.

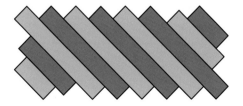

4. Trim the block to 5½" x 15", keeping the strips at an approximate 45° angle.

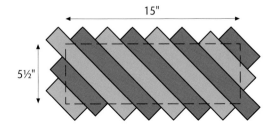

15"

5½"

5. Repeat steps 1–4 to create a total of three pieced rectangles.

ADDING THE SPOTS

1. Using the spot pattern on page 54, trace four spots onto each 5½" x 15" background rectangle, staggering them along the length of the rectangle. Cut out inside the circles, ¼" from the drawn lines, and clip into the seam allowance every ¼" almost to the drawn line.

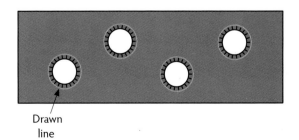

Drawn line

2. Sew the pieced rectangles to the background rectangles as shown.

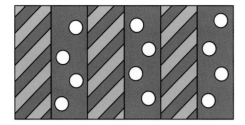

3. Referring to "Reverse Appliqué" on page 75, layer the table-runner top on the batting if desired. Place the 5" x 14½" rectangles underneath each of the background rectangles, ensuring that all the openings have adequate fabric underneath. Pin throughout the background rectangles to secure the three layers.

4. Hand sew the spots using reverse appliqué.

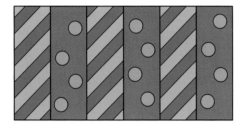

FINISHING

1. Baste the table-runner top, batting, and backing fabric. Quilt as desired. I free-motion machine quilted a spiral within each spot, meandering in the spot backgrounds, and zigzags in each strip, matching the thread colors to the fabric.

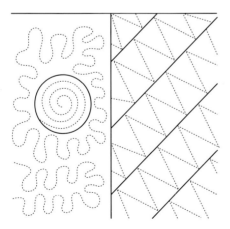

2. Stitch the binding strips into one continuous strip and bind your table runner.

Amber Glow

This version of the table runner uses four matching colors for the spots and stripes, blending the overall surface a bit more. You could use just two colors for the spots and match them to the stripes, or go for even more than four.

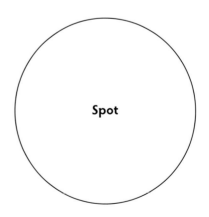

Spot

Little Log Cabin Coasters

FINISHED COASTER: 5½" x 5½"

I don't use a lot of traditional quilting designs in my work, but I make an exception for the Log Cabin. I love this quintessential quilt block and the way it's open to improvisation and irregularity—and, of course, the fact that it's composed of basic geometric shapes. By varying the color of the central square and the order of the surrounding strips, you can create a cohesive set in which each coaster is still unique. There's nothing like colorful coasters to make happy hour even happier.

MATERIALS FOR 6 COASTERS

Yardage is based on 42"-wide fabric.

¼ yard *each* of 6 different solid fabrics for coaster tops and backs: orange, magenta, aqua, red, purple, and green in the coasters shown
⅔ yard of medium-weight, 20"-wide interfacing
6 squares, 7" x 7", of batting*

A firm, low-loft batting is best for coasters.

CUTTING

Cut your fabrics randomly, varying the exact sizes of the center squares and the widths of the strips. Use the sizes listed as a rough guide, with the exception of the square for the backing, which should be at least 7"x 7".

From *each* of the 6 solid fabrics, cut:
1 square, ranging from 2" x 2" to 2½" x 2½"
2 strips, ranging from 1½" to 2" x 42"
1 square, 7" x 7"

From the interfacing, cut:
6 squares, 7" x 7"

ASSEMBLING THE COASTERS

You will use a different-colored square for the center of each coaster, surrounding it with strips of the five other colors. Arrange and sew the colors sequentially, starting with a strip of color 1, then 2, 3, 4, and 5, and starting again at 1. Vary the order of colors with each coaster. You will trim the strips to the correct lengths as you go. When sewing, make sure the center squares and strips are wide enough so that you will be able to cut a square, 6" x 6", from the finished Log Cabin.

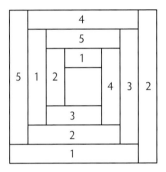

1. Sew a strip to the edge of a square. Trim the strip even with the square, and press the seam allowances open or away from the square.

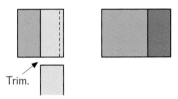

Trim.

2. Working counterclockwise, sew a strip of a second color to the next edge of the unit; trim and press as before.

3. Continue sewing strips in this manner, adding each strip to the side perpendicular to the strip just sewn and working in a counterclockwise direction, until the center square is surrounded by three strips on each side.

4. Repeat steps 1–3 to make a total of six coasters. Trim each one to 6" x 6".

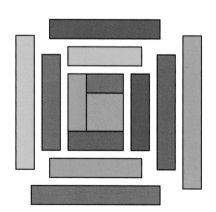

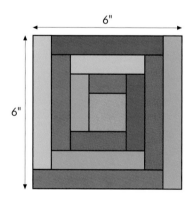

FINISHING

1. Layer the batting, interfacing, and backing right side up; place the trimmed Log Cabin block on top with the wrong side up. Pin through all four layers. I matched the backing color to the center square of the coaster top, but you can distribute the colors however you like. Repeat for each block.

2. Sew around the perimeter of each block using a ¼" seam allowance and leaving a 3" opening in the middle of one side.

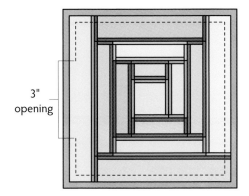

3"
opening

3. Trim the excess batting, backing fabric, and interfacing even with the pieced blocks. Trim across each of the four corners and turn the coasters right side out through the opening. Push out the corners with a blunt-pointed object, and slip-stitch the opening closed using matching thread.

4. Quilt each coaster as desired. I free-motion machine stitched a square spiral, matching the thread color to the fabric of the center square.

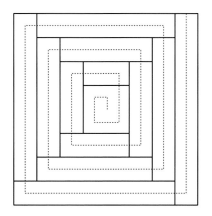

···· **Spiraling Solids** ························

Instead of using the same six colors throughout the set, I composed each of these coasters from shades of the same hue. The result is still a cohesive collection, but with more contrast between the individual coasters.

Woven Patchwork Place Mats

FINISHED PLACE MAT: 19½" x 15½"

When I was growing up, my mother always considered mealtime a respected respite toward the end of the day. It was a chance to sit down as a family, and setting the table with place mats was a regular part of that routine. They're a great way to jazz up your table for a dinner party, or even an everyday meal, adding character and a celebratory feel no matter the occasion. The arrangement of the strips in this design creates a woven, overlapping effect. This is another one of those great projects for gobbling up your stash, since you can use whatever colors you like for the squares.

MATERIALS FOR 4 PLACE MATS

Yardage is based on 42"-wide fabric.

1 yard *total* of assorted solid fabrics for squares
    OR 1 fat eighth *each* of 10 different solid fabrics
½ yard of charcoal fabric for vertical strips
½ yard of gray fabric for horizontal strips
1½ yards of solid fabric for backing
¼ yard *each* of 4 different solid fabrics for binding: neon green, coral, orange, and blue in the place mats shown
4 pieces, 20" x 24", of batting

CUTTING

From the assorted solid fabrics, cut:
80 squares, 3½" x 3½"

From the charcoal fabric, cut:
10 strips, 1½" x 42"

From the gray fabric, cut:
10 strips, 1½" x 42"

From *each* of the 4 binding fabrics, cut:
2 strips, 2" x 42"

From the backing fabric, cut:
2 strips, 24" x 42"; cut into 4 rectangles, 24" x 20"

ASSEMBLING THE PLACE MATS

Each place mat is composed of four different sections. Mix up the colors of the squares and trim the strips as you go, rather than measuring and cutting them all beforehand. Before pressing the seam allowances, simply trim off the excess strip by cutting along the edge of the square.

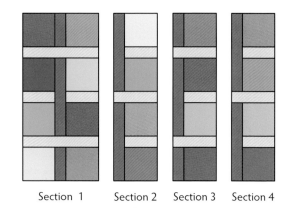

Section 1   Section 2   Section 3   Section 4

Section 1

1. Sew one 3½" square to a charcoal strip. Trim off the excess strip fabric, press the seam allowances open, and sew another 3½" square to the opposite side of the strip. Make two of these units with a charcoal strip and two with a gray strip.

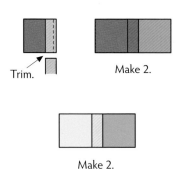

Trim.   Make 2.

Make 2.

2. Sew a gray strip to the long edge of each charcoal unit from step 1. Trim off the excess gray strip.

Make 2.

3. Sew a charcoal strip to the long edge of one gray unit from step 1. Trim off the excess charcoal strip. Sew the remaining gray unit to the other side of the charcoal strip.

4. Sew the units from steps 2 and 3 together as shown to make section 1.

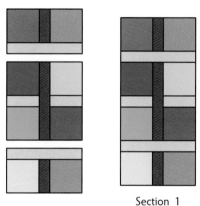

Section 1

Sections 2 and 4

1. Sew two units consisting of two squares, one short gray strip, and a long charcoal strip on one of the long edges. These units are the same as those created in steps 1 and 2 of section 1, except that the colors of the strips are reversed; the short strip is gray and the long strip is charcoal.

Make 2.

2. Sew a gray strip to the short edge of one of the units from step 1, positioning the long charcoal strip on the left.

Make 1.

3. Sew the units from steps 1 and 2 together as shown to make section 2.

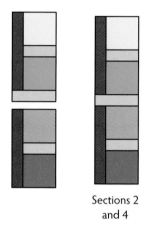

Sections 2 and 4

4. Repeat steps 1–3 to make section 4.

Section 3

1. Sew a charcoal strip to one side of a square and trim. Make two of these units.

Make 2.

2. Sew together two squares, a short gray strip, and a long charcoal strip as shown. Sew a gray strip to each short edge of the unit, positioning the charcoal strip on the left.

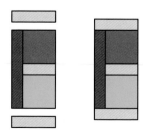

3. Sew the units from steps 1 and 2 together as shown to make section 3.

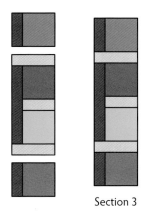

Section 3

Joining the Sections

Sew the sections together, lining up the seams to create the woven effect.

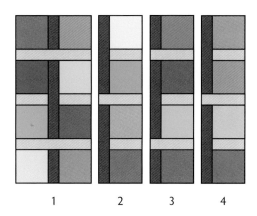

1   2   3   4

FINISHING

1. Baste the place mats and quilt as desired. I free-motion machine stitched a square spiral in each square using beige thread, and an undulating line in the woven strips with matching gray and charcoal thread.

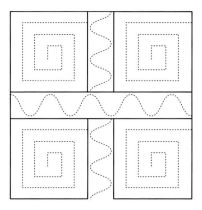

2. Stitch the binding strips for each place mat together to make a continuous strip and bind your place mats.

Black and Bright

This place mat reverses the areas of color and neutral, with all the squares black and the strips in alternating colors. Zigzag quilting in each square and swirly stitches in the strips create an alternative texture. You could also try using just two different colors for the squares, or just four or five—each approach will transform the finished result.

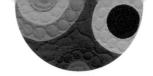

Dancing Dots Table Topper

FINISHED QUILT: 30" DIAMETER

I always try to have a hand-stitching project to work on, in case I find myself faced with a long trip by car or plane, or if I just want to unwind in front of the television with needle and thread. This little quilt is perfect for fulfilling that requirement—it's not too big to carry around, but lots of hand stitching is involved. It's also a wonderful scrap-busting project, enabling you to use up some of those itty-bitty leftover pieces of fabric. The circular shape accentuates the fun, bubbly pattern, and it's the perfect size for a baby quilt, wall quilt, or even a table topper.

MATERIALS

Yardage is based on 42"-wide fabric.

1 yard of solid fabric for background: orange in the quilt shown

1¼ yards *total* of scraps, 2" to 6" square, of assorted solid fabrics for circles: blue, light blue, aqua, dark blue, turquoise, green, lime green, mint green, dark green, light orange, violet, purple, dark purple, plum, magenta, yellow, pink, light pink, dark pink, red, and brick red in the quilt shown

¼ yard of lime-green fabric for binding

1¼ yards of flannel for backing

38" x 38" piece of batting

Template plastic

Fabric pen or pencil

CUTTING

Make templates using the circle patterns on page 66. Trace the circles onto selected fabrics; add a ¼" seam allowance outside of the marked line when cutting. Because some of circles 1–6 will be reverse appliquéd, add a ½" seam allowance outside of the marked line when cutting; if you end up stitching them using regular appliqué, simply trim the seam allowance as you work. Feel free to vary the number and size of circles as desired.

From the fabric scraps, cut:
6 of circle 1
10 of circle 2
13 of circle 3
10 of circle 4
14 of circle 5
13 of circle 6
5 of circle 7

From the background fabric, cut:
1 circle, 30" in diameter*

From the binding fabric, cut:
3 strips, 2" x 42"

From the backing fabric, cut:
1 circle, 38" in diameter*

See "Cutting Large Circles" on page 64 for detailed instructions.

Cutting Large Circles

I find that the easiest way to cut a large circle from fabric is to fold the fabric in half, and then in half again. From the folded corner, measure out the radius of the circle (in this case, 15" for the background and 19" for the backing). Mark this distance several times on the fabric. Draw a curved line through these marks. Cut along the curved line through all four layers to create the circle.

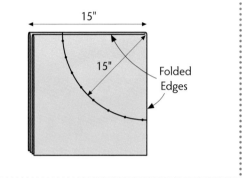

APPLIQUÉING THE QUILT TOP

The circles are appliquéd using hand appliqué and reverse appliqué. The largest circles in each "stack" are hand appliquéd, the second circles are reverse appliquéd, and the third circles (when added) are hand appliquéd. Refer to "Hand Appliqué" on page 73 and "Reverse Appliqué" on page 75 for additional details.

1. Lay the background fabric on top of the batting, if desired, and smooth or iron it out.

2. Starting in the center of the quilt top, layer and pin the circles onto the background. Refer to the diagram at right as a general guideline for placement or arrange the circles as you like. As you arrange the circles, you will need to cut out the reverse-appliqué interiors. (I like to do this as I go, but you could also cut them all out beforehand.) To do this, trace the template of the second circle onto the larger circle, and cut out ¼" within the drawn line. Clip into the seam allowance every ¼" almost to the marked line.

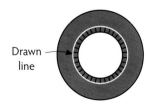

3. For each of the two-layer stacks, position the outer color, and then layer the second color underneath and in the center. Place the three-layer stacks in the same manner, adding the third circle in the middle of the second. Pin the circles securely in place.

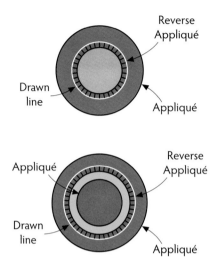

4. Once you have arranged all the circles on the quilt top, stitch them in place using hand appliqué and reverse appliqué.

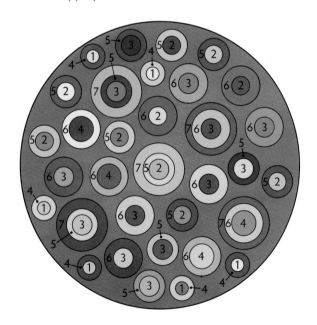

FINISHING

1. Baste your quilt and quilt as desired. I free-motion machine stitched a spiral within each center circle and stitched small circles in the outer rings, matching the thread color to the fabric. I also stitched loose waves on the background between the circles.

2. Stitch the binding strips into one continuous strip and bind your quilt, curving the binding to line up with the curved quilt circumference as you stitch it in place. Some quilters prefer cutting bias binding to use on curved edges, but I find you can get away without it in this case.

···· Night and Day ····················

The primarily neutral palette of this quilt makes the select spots of color really pop and adds an element of contrast to the design. You could also try using different values of the same hue in each circle, or use the same hue in all the circles for a more cohesive quilt top.

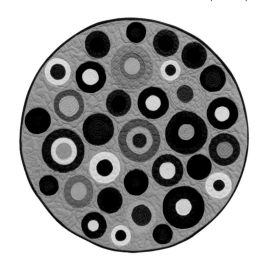

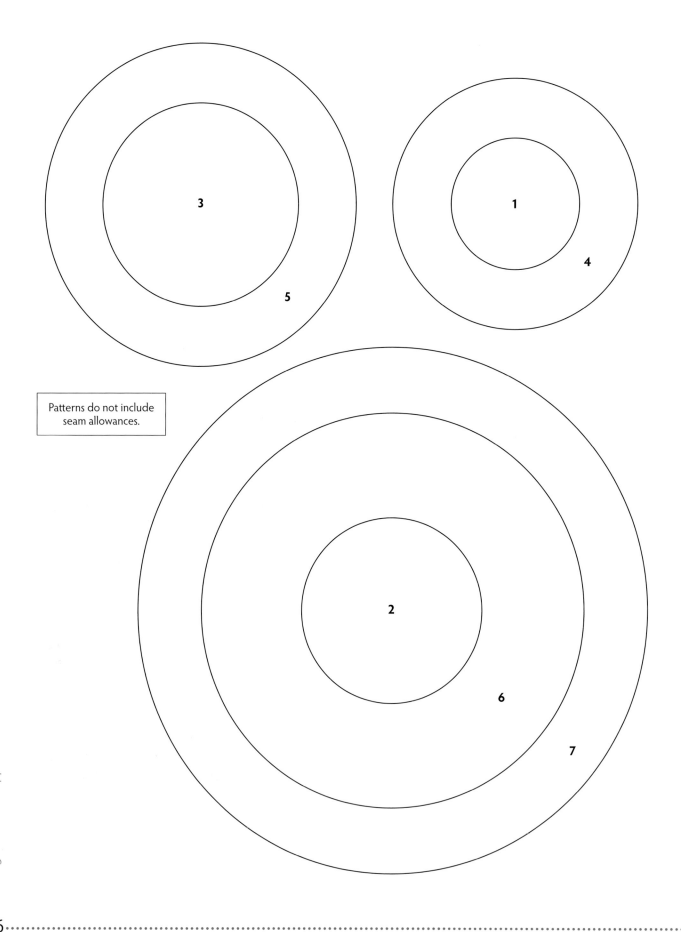

Patterns do not include seam allowances.

Shifting Stripes Rug

FINISHED RUG: 21½" x 37½"

Quilts show up in all kinds of places these days—walls, tabletops, sofas, etc.—but you don't often see them on the floor. I figured, why not? This little rug lives right next to my bed where it doesn't get heavy use—just socks and slippers. It's composed of lots of narrow strips, so it's perfect for using scraps and bits of fabric that you already have on hand. I find that working with such narrow strips often results in some wonkiness—the stripes tend to curve a bit—so embrace it! To truly emphasize the scrappiness, I like to use lots of short strips for the binding as well.

MATERIALS

Yardage is based on 42"-wide fabric.

1⅔ yards *total* of assorted solid scraps for stripes, spots, and binding*

25" x 42" piece of heavyweight cotton fabric for backing

25" x 42" piece of batting**

Template plastic

Fabric pen or pencil

*Include as many colors as possible; the rug shown contains about 20 different colors.

**Use a firm batting with body such as needle-punched cotton for a rug, rather than one that is soft and drapey.

CUTTING

Make a full circle template using the half-circle pattern on page 70. Trace the circle onto selected fabrics; add a ¼" seam allowance outside of the marked line when cutting.

From the assorted scraps, cut:*

4 strips, 1½" x 6"
4 strips, 1½" x 7"
8 strips, 1½" x 8"
2 strips, 1½" x 11½"
5 strips, 1½" x 15¼"
2 strips, 1½" x 18"
4 strips, 1½" x 20"
3 strips, 1½" x 22¾"
2 strips, 1½" x 25½"
7 strips, 1½" x 30"
2 strips, 1½" x 32"
2 strips, 1½" x 37½"
6 circles
28 binding strips, 2" x 6", or 2"-wide strips to total an approximate length of 132"

*You may want to wait and cut some of your strips as you sew; that way you can choose the colors that will go next to each other.

ASSEMBLING THE RUG TOP

It is easiest to piece the top in sections. You can cut all the strip lengths beforehand for random color placement, or cut the lengths as you go to determine color placement when sewing.

Section 1

1. Sew four 8" strips together along their long edges.
2. Sew four 30" strips together along their long edges.

3. Sew the 8" unit to the 30" unit along their short edges, lining up the seams.

4. Sew one 37½" strip to the unit from step 3, positioning the 8" unit on the left.

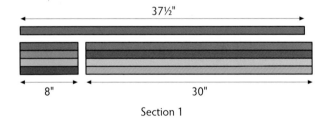

Section 1

Section 2

1. Sew two 15¼" strips together along their short edges to make a 30" strip.

2. Sew three 30" strips together along their long edges. Sew the strip from step 1 to the bottom of this unit.

3. Sew four 8" strips together along their long edges.

4. Sew the units from steps 2 and 3 together as shown.

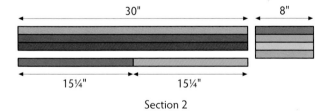

Section 2

Section 3

1. Sew three 15¼" strips together along their long edges.
2. Sew three 22¾" strips together along their long edges.
3. Sew the units from steps 1 and 2 together as shown.

Section 3

Section 4

1. Sew two 7" strips together along their long edges.
2. Sew two 25½" strips together along their long edges.
3. Sew the units from steps 1 and 2 together along their short edges.
4. Sew two 32" strips together along their long edges.
5. Sew the unit from step 3 to the unit from step 4, positioning the 7" unit on the right.
6. Sew four 6" strips together along their long edges. Sew this unit to the unit from step 5 along their short edges as shown.

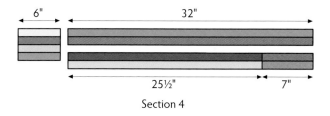

Section 4

Section 5

1. Sew two 7" strips together along their long edges.
2. Sew two 11½" strips together along their long edges.
3. Sew the units from steps 1 and 2 together along their short edges.
4. Sew two 18" strips together along their long edges.
5. Sew the units from steps 3 and 4 together along their long edges, positioning the 7" unit on the right.
6. Sew four 20" strips together along their long edges.
7. Sew the units from steps 5 and 6 together along their short edges.

8. Sew a 37½" strip to the bottom edge of the unit from step 7.

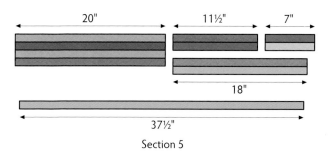

Section 5

Joining the Sections

Sew sections 1–5 together, starting with sections 1 and 2, and then adding sections 3, 4, and 5.

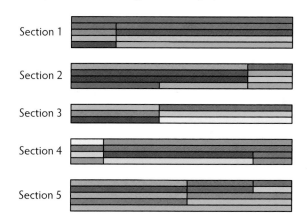

APPLIQUÉING THE CIRCLES

1. Referring to "Hand Appliqué" on page 73, arrange the six circles on the quilt top, centering them over the six areas where four seams meet, as shown in the diagram. Pin the circles in position, ensuring that the top is smooth.
2. Stitch the circles in place by hand.

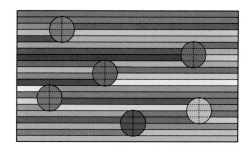

FINISHING

1. Baste the rug and quilt as desired. I machine quilted vertical lines about 1" apart across the entire rug top, alternating between four different thread colors. I used a universal needle and a slightly longer stitch length when quilting the rug since it's thicker than most projects.

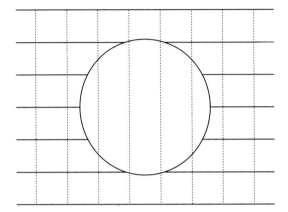

2. Sew the assorted 2"-wide binding strips together to make one continuous strip that is approximately 132" long. Bind your rug.

···· Eclipsed Rainbows ········

Through the use of a single range of hues in different areas of the quilt, the shifting quality of the stripes becomes even more apparent. Swirly quilting on the stripes and a zigzag pattern on the circles focus more attention on the individual motifs and specific areas of the quilt.

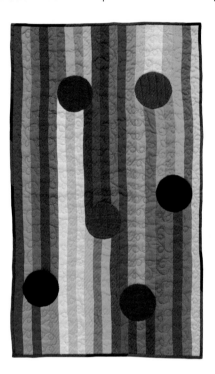

> Pattern does not include seam allowance.

Rotate and align pattern on dashed line to make full circle pattern.

Half circle

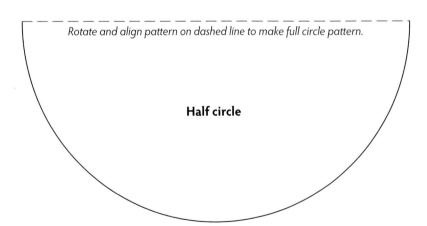

Quiltmaking Basics

In this section, I discuss the basics of quiltmaking so that if you're a beginner, you should be able to tackle all of the projects in this book. Some of my quiltmaking techniques may be a bit unconventional, but they work for me. There are many ways to achieve the same end result, and many helpful quiltmaking resources, so if you prefer a different method, by all means, go for it.

FIGURING OUT FABRIC

Most quilting fabric is 100% cotton, sold off a bolt, and is 42" to 44" wide. The selvage edges are the finished edges of the fabric; they run along the length of the fabric and should be cut off before you begin working. Note that when you work with solid-colored fabrics, both sides of the fabric are the same; there's no right or wrong side to worry about.

Fabric has three grains. The crosswise grain runs perpendicular to the selvage, and the lengthwise grain runs parallel to it. The bias grain runs at a 45° angle across the fabric.

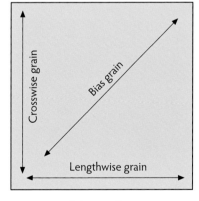

Selvage edge

Crosswise grain

Bias grain

Lengthwise grain

Selvage edge

The lengthwise grain has the least amount of stretch, the crosswise grain has a bit more stretch, and bias has the most stretch. It is best to cut your binding fabric along the crosswise grain, and to cut geometric shapes, such as squares and stripes, perpendicular to the lengthwise and crosswise grains. Many quilters cut along the bias for binding strips, especially if a quilt has curved edges, but I find that the crosswise grain works just fine.

Fabric sold off the bolt is measured by yards. Fabric can also be sold as fat quarters, which are pieces measuring 18" x 21" instead of the typical ¼-yard cut of 9" x 42". All calculations for cutting and yardage in this book are based on 42"-wide fabric, with 40" of useable width after prewashing and removing selvages.

Whether or not to wash your fabric beforehand is a matter of personal preference. Many quilters prefer doing so in order to remove any excess dye and to preshrink the fabric. I find that you can get away with either; just be prepared for a slightly "puckered" quilt if you wash it after quilting. If you do choose to wash your fabric, launder it in the washing machine with warm water and mild detergent. Dry fabric on a low or medium setting and press to remove wrinkles.

Flannel Backings

I like to use flannel fabric for the backing of my quilts and pillows. It emphasizes one of my favorite aspects of these items—that they're meant to be used and cuddled up under. I often use solid tones such as brown or black, but flannels are also available in other solid colors and in many different colorful prints. Flannel tends to shrink more than regular quilting cottons, so it's best to prewash and preshrink flannel before using it.

THE QUILTER'S TOOLBOX

All quilters have favorite quilting tools and supplies based on their unique needs and preferences. There are, however, some essentials that you should always have on hand.

Sewing machine. There are countless brands and types of sewing machines, but it all boils down to personal preference. Choosing a sewing machine is a serious undertaking; do some research and try out different machines to ensure you make the right investment for you.

Rotary cutter and mat. The standard-sized rotary cutter is 45 mm. You may also want to invest in a smaller size and a larger size. When it comes to rotary-cutting mats, larger is better; give yourself plenty of working space.

Acrylic ruler. I recommend having a variety of rulers. A 6" x 24" or 6½" x 24" ruler is good for straightening fabric and cutting strips. In addition, I'd suggest a large 12½" x 12½" square ruler, a 3" x 18" ruler, and a small 3" x 3" square. This makes it easy to cut a range of shapes and sizes from your fabric.

Scissors. You'll want a couple pairs of scissors for the different aspects of your work, including a large pair for cutting fabric and a small, sharp pair for hand appliqué and clipping threads. It's also a good idea to have a pair of craft scissors for cutting paper and template plastic.

Iron and ironing board. Any standard iron and board will suffice. I like having a smaller tabletop ironing board to keep on my sewing table while I work, and a larger freestanding one for pressing larger pieces of fabric.

Seam ripper. Trust me, this will alleviate a lot of stress when you realize you've mis-stitched a piece of fabric . . . or several.

Pins. Long pins are best for securing larger pieces of fabric, while shorter and smaller pins are better for appliqué work.

Needles. You'll want a variety of types and sizes for your sewing machine and for hand stitching. I use universal or Sharp/Microtex needles in my machine, and Sharps or quilting needles when stitching by hand.

Thread. I use all-purpose 100% cotton thread for most of my piecing, machine quilting, and appliqué. However, there are many different types of threads that are nice for machine quilting, including rayon and metallic. Silk thread is wonderful for hand appliqué. Experiment to find what type you prefer.

Fabric-marking pencils or pens. It's helpful to have both light and dark colors for marking different shades of fabric. Always test your marker on the fabric beforehand to ensure that it will wash out.

ROTARY CUTTING

When it comes to cutting your fabrics, rotary cutters make life a whole lot easier—they're great for cutting straight edges, and even for cutting through multiple layers at once. Working with rotary cutters does take some practice, but trust me—once you get the feel for it, it's much quicker and more efficient than using scissors.

Typically when rotary cutting strips, squares, and rectangles, you will cut fabric along the straight grain. Before you begin cutting, make sure the fabric is well pressed to ensure accuracy. Place your fabric on your rotary-cutting mat and hold the ruler over it, pressing down on the ruler with your left hand (or vice versa if you are left-handed). Be sure to press firmly so the ruler doesn't slide as you cut; some rulers have nonskid bottoms to help prevent this. Hold the rotary cutter firmly in your dominant hand, with the fabric and ruler in front of you. Slide the rotary cutter along the edge of the ruler to cut through your fabric.

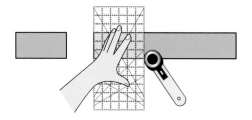

····· **Cut with Caution** ·····················

For safety, it's best to stand when rotary cutting, and it's easiest on your back to have a cutting surface at about the height of a kitchen counter. Move slowly and carefully when working with a rotary cutter, and always cut *away* from you; never pull the cutter toward you. A rotary cutter is a very sharp tool, so take your time. Change your rotary blade frequently, every month or so depending on how much cutting you're doing. This ensures that it will glide easily through the fabric, resulting in a nice, clean cut.

PIECING

The process of piecing, also known as patchwork, is the most basic quiltmaking technique, and it's more than a little addictive. Watching a quilt top come to life as you combine various bits of fabric step by step is immensely gratifying.

All the projects in this book use a ¼" seam allowance for piecing. I always do my piecing by machine, using a stitch length of 2.4, but you can piece by hand if you prefer.

When sewing together two pieces of fabric, layer them one on top of the other with their right sides facing. (Remember that solids do not have right and wrong sides.) Pin the two pieces together if desired; you may find that you don't need to pin smaller pieces. Using a straight stitch, sew ¼" from the pinned edges of the fabrics, removing the pins as you get to them. I like to backstitch once or twice at the beginning and end of the stitching, but it's not essential, as the stitching will eventually be crossed by other stitching.

Always press your seams as you work. This ensures that the fabric lies as flat as possible. I press all seam allowances open because it makes a flatter quilt top and there is less bulk in the seam allowances. If you want added dimension on one side of the seam or the other, press the seam allowances to one side. You can wait and press a few seams at the same time; just be sure that you always press seam allowances open before sewing across them.

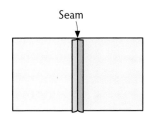

Seam

APPLIQUÉ

I used to find appliqué intimidating, but it's surprisingly fun and easy once you get the hang of it. It's also one of the easiest ways to incorporate curved shapes into your quilt designs, breaking free from the geometric limitations of patchwork alone. Appliqué refers to sewing one piece of fabric on top of another, while reverse appliqué involves cutting into a top fabric and inserting a fabric layer underneath. These approaches have different textural and visual effects; I love using a combination of appliqué and reverse appliqué to achieve circular motifs with layers and dimension.

All my appliqué is done by hand. I find it to be a nice change of pace from machine stitching, a bit more methodical, slow-paced, and soothing—plus it's portable! I never go on vacation without an appliqué project in my bag. And I find there's no better way to unwind at the end of the day, whether it's hand stitching in front of the TV or over drinks with a friend.

Sometimes I like some extra support when doing reverse appliqué, so I'll stitch with the quilt top's background fabric pin basted to the batting. All the reverse appliqué in this book is done on a whole-cloth background, or a quilt top that has already been pieced together, so you may choose to appliqué with the batting if you like. I begin the appliqué by stitching the shapes on the outer edges of the quilt top first, and then I work my way toward the center.

···· Making Templates for Appliqué ········

The appliqué shapes in this book are all circular pattern pieces. To create templates from these patterns, photocopy them, and then trace them onto template plastic and cut out the shape on the drawn line. If you use translucent template plastic, you can trace directly from the book pages.

Hand Appliqué

Use thread that matches the color of your fabric so that your stitches won't show. I use a small, sharp hand-sewing needle such as a quilting needle (called a Between), or a Sharp. Some quilters prefer a longer needle for appliqué, such as a milliner's needle or straw needle.

1. To prepare the piece for appliqué, trace the template onto your appliqué fabric (if using a print rather than a solid, trace onto the fabric's right side) and cut out the shape, adding approximately ¼" outside of the drawn line for a seam allowance.

quiltmaking basics

2. Lay the appliqué on top of the background fabric. Pin it in place using straight pins or small appliqué pins, depending on the size of the shape; be sure to pin both in the center and around the edge, allowing enough space near the drawn line for turning under and stitching.

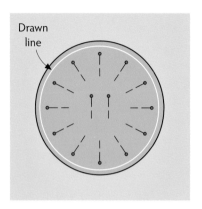

3. Cut a piece of thread approximately 18" long. Thread your needle and knot the end. Insert the threaded needle into the back of the appliqué piece so that it comes out on the front just inside the drawn line. This will hide the knot underneath the appliqué piece when you're done turning and stitching.

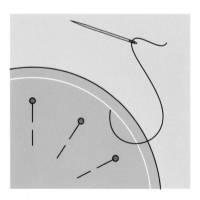

4. Fold the edge of the appliqué piece under along the drawn line about ½" to 1" ahead of your needle. Be sure that the drawn line is turned under and is not visible at the fold. Insert the needle into the background fabric next to the folded edge of the appliqué and then bring it through the folded edge of the appliqué piece about ⅛" away. Take small stitches every ⅛", catching just the edge of

the folded fabric. If you're right-handed, you'll be working counterclockwise; left-handed stitchers will work clockwise. Continue in this manner, folding under along the drawn line as you go.

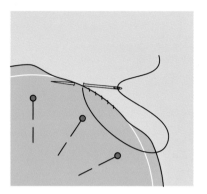

···· **Folding the Fabric Under** ················

You can use the needle to turn the fabric under as you stitch. This process is called needle-turn appliqué. I prefer to fold with my fingers. But you should try both methods to see what works best for you.

5. When you have stitched around the entire shape, take a few more stitches past the starting point for extra security. Take the needle to the wrong side of the work and loop through one of the appliqué stitches; knot around it twice. Insert the needle underneath the appliqué piece and bring it back up a couple inches from the knotted edge, pulling the thread through the background fabric. Trim off the excess thread.

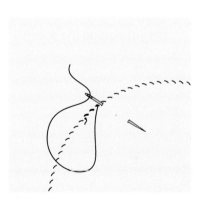

Reverse Appliqué

The reverse appliqué in this book is used either to create several circles on a whole-cloth background, or to create small circles within larger appliquéd circles. While the extra support of batting isn't necessary for regular appliqué, I find it very helpful for the reverse method.

1. To prepare for reverse appliqué, trace the template onto the wrong side of your background fabric. Cut out *inside* the drawn line, leaving a seam allowance of about ¼". Clip into the seam allowance every ¼" or so *almost* to the drawn line.

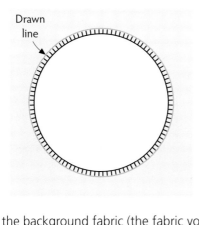

Drawn line

2. Layer the background fabric (the fabric you have cut into) onto the batting. Insert the appliqué fabric so it is centered under the cut opening. Pin in the center through the fabric and batting, and pin around the edges through both layers of fabric and batting. Be sure to leave space for turning the fabric under and sewing.

3. Cut a piece of thread approximately 18" long. Thread your needle and knot the end. Insert the threaded needle into the batting, through the appliqué piece, and into the background so that it exits just outside the drawn line (the unclipped side).

4. Fold under ½" to 1" of the snipped seam. Insert the needle into the appliqué fabric next to the folded edge of the background and then bring it through the folded edge again about ⅛" away, catching just the edge of the folded fabric. Take small stitches every ⅛" and continue around the circle as in step 4 of, "Hand Appliqué," opposite. For reverse appliqué, you will be stitching in

a clockwise direction if you're right-handed and counterclockwise if you're left-handed.

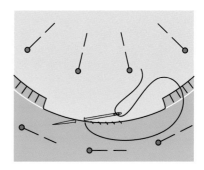

5. Finish and knot in the same manner as for hand appliqué.

····· **Combining Appliqué Techniques** ·········

A couple of the projects in this book involve stitching reverse-appliqué circles in the middle of larger appliquéd circles. In these cases, I find it easiest to do the reverse appliqué first and then appliqué the entire unit in place. The interior stitches anchor the fabric and make it easier to stitch the outer edges.

FINISHING AND BINDING

I've never understood why some quilters dread the final stages of the quiltmaking process. Of course, assembling a quilt top is exciting and gratifying, but I also love the sense of completion and accomplishment that comes with finishing up a project. The slow, steady process of basting, the added dimension of quilting stitches, and incorporating that last little dose of color in the binding—these steps are like icing the cake.

Basting

Before quilting, you need to secure the three layers: backing fabric, batting, and quilt top. This creates a quilt "sandwich." Always layer the backing fabric wrong side up, add the batting, and then add the quilt top right side up. Make sure that all three layers are completely smoothed out and free of wrinkles. I sometimes like to iron the quilt top once I've laid it on top of the batting, just to be safe. You will have extra batting and backing fabric on each side; it's important to have some wiggle room when quilting.

I usually do machine quilting and baste with safety pins. Insert the pins every 3" to 5" depending on the size of the project, pinning through all three layers and working from the center of the quilt out to the edges. For hand quilting, baste by sewing long hand stitches through all three layers.

Quilting

Quilting refers to the process of stitching through all three layers of the quilt in order to hold the layers together. It's a wonderful and unique part of the quilt-making process. Quilting stitches add an additional layer of pattern, dimension, and color to our work. I always feel like this stage of quilt creation is what brings my projects to life.

You can quilt either by hand or by machine. I occasionally hand quilt a project if I want to take it with me when I travel, or if I'm craving some slow-paced handwork, but the majority of my pieces are machine quilted.

You can use a variety of threads when machine quilting; just be sure to match the top and bobbin threads in materials, strength, and weight. I most often match my bobbin thread to the color of the backing fabric, but you may also choose to match the top and bobbin thread colors to hide any stitch-tension irregularities.

Machine quilting falls into two main categories: straight-line and free-motion.

Straight-line machine quilting. This method of quilting is just what it sounds like—quilting through the quilt top with straight lines, which can run horizontally, vertically, or diagonally. When machine stitching straight lines, use a walking foot; this helps to feed the layers of the quilt sandwich along evenly. I set my stitch length to 4.0 for straight stitching (about nine stitches per inch).

You can use straight lines to stitch any number of designs, including grids of diamonds or squares. You can also simply quilt in the seams of the patchwork, called quilting "in the ditch," or quilt ¼" from the seams, called "outline quilting."

Free-motion machine quilting. Free-motion machine quilting basically allows you to draw with your needle, stitching any shapes you like. This is very freeing, but it takes quite a lot of practice. In order to free-motion stitch, you will need to drop your feed dogs, or the teeth that feed your fabric through the machine; you are then able to move your quilt underneath the needle—in any direction.

You will need a free-motion or darning foot. My stitch length ranges from 3.5 to 4.0 when free-motion quilting, depending on the size of the project and quilting motifs. Figuring out the correct speed and rhythm for moving your quilt under the needle takes time; when it comes to free-motion work, there's no substitute for continuous practice and patience! I suggest making several practice quilt sandwiches. You may also want to consider taking a class at a nearby quilt shop, or refer to the many helpful online and print resources available on the subject.

Quilting motifs. The possibilities of quilting motifs are endless. Different designs will transform your quilt top in unique ways, so have fun trying out a variety of approaches. I find that my quilting patterns fall into two main categories: smaller patterns stitched within each shape on the quilt top, or an overall pattern that covers the entire design. The former approach requires more stopping and cutting but draws focus to individual segments of the quilt top; the latter will add greater visual cohesion to the design.

The degree to which you plan out your quilting stitches is also up to you. Some quilters choose to draw the motifs onto the quilt top beforehand, but I prefer a more freewheeling approach guided by the shapes and design of the quilt top. If you are quilting a design that you do not want to be cut off at the edges, leave at least ¼" unquilted along the edge of the quilt to allow for the binding.

You can also choose matching or contrasting threads when quilting. Matching your threads will draw the focus to the shape and dimensionality of the stitches, while contrasting threads will add another element of color to your work.

Achieving the correct thread tension is one of the trickiest aspects of machine quilting. I've been quilting for several years, and I still struggle with this. You know you have the correct tension when none of the bobbin thread is visible on the top of the quilt, and none of the top thread is visible on the back. Depending on the project and the type of thread you're using, you'll need to experiment with different top and bottom tensions until you have achieved the correct balance. Before beginning to quilt on your final piece, practice on a small sandwich with the same backing, batting, and top fabric to adjust the thread tension.

If the top tension is too tight, the lower thread is pulled toward the right side of the fabric; try lowering the tension.

If the top tension is too loose, the upper thread is pulled toward the back side of the sandwich; try increasing the tension.

Occasionally, you may find that you need to adjust the bobbin tension. This is done by turning the little screw on your bobbin case *very slightly,* either to the right to tighten it or to the left to loosen it. Your bobbin should sit securely in the bobbin case. If it slides easily, try tightening the screw; if it is difficult to remove, loosen the screw.

Binding

There are several ways to bind a quilt, but the instructions here are for a continuous strip of double-fold binding with mitered corners. All the projects in this book have a binding that finishes approximately ¼" wide, but you may prefer a wider binding; if so, be sure to cut your strips wider than the suggested 2". The yardage calculations include enough extra to accommodate cutting wider binding strips.

1. Trim the excess batting and backing fabric even with the quilt top.

2. Cut the required number of binding strips along the crosswise grain. To create one continuous strip, lay the ends of two of the strips perpendicular to one another with right sides facing and sew along the diagonal. Trim the seam allowances to ¼" and press them open. Repeat until you have sewn together all of the strips.

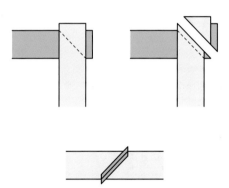

3. Fold the binding in half lengthwise with wrong sides together and press.

4. Line up the raw edges of the binding with the raw edge of the quilt, with the quilt top facing up. (You can pin or just line up the raw edges as you go; I prefer not to pin.) Leaving roughly 8" of unsewn binding at the start, sew the binding to the quilt using a ¼" seam allowance, stopping ¼" before the corner. Backsitch and cut the thread.

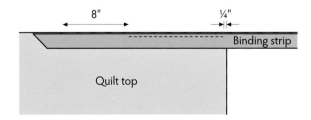

5. Rotate the quilt so that the next side to be sewn is perpendicular to you. Fold the binding strip upward so the raw edges are lined up with the raw quilt edge about to be sewn, and then fold it back toward you, aligning the raw edges of the binding and quilt as before. Start sewing ¼" from the corner. Take a couple of stitches, then back-stitch and continue.

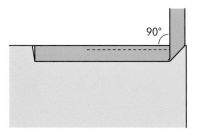

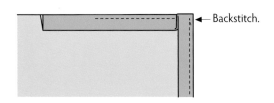

← Backstitch.

6. Continue in this manner until you are about 10" from where you started sewing. Cut your threads.

7. Fold back the two loose ends of binding fabric so the folds meet, and press the folds.

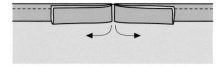

8. Cut *one* of the loose binding ends along the ironed fold, and cut the other 2" from the ironed fold so that it is longer than the other loose binding end. (If you cut your binding wider than 2", use that dimension.) Fold back the ends of the binding at 45° angles and press the folds. Pin the ends right sides together along the ironed fold and stitch on the fold. Press the seam allowances open.

Unfinished quilt edge

9. Finish stitching the binding to the quilt.

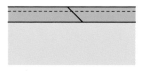

10. Before turning the binding to the back of the quilt, fold the raw edge over so that it meets the stitching line. Press the fold and then turn the binding to the back of the quilt. Pin the binding to the back of the quilt, and slip-stitch the folded edge in place, stitching through the folded edge of the binding strip, the backing fabric, and the batting.

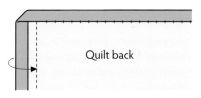

Quilt back

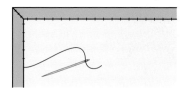

Hand stitch binding to quilt back.

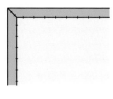

Acknowledgments

Throughout the course of writing this book, I've been constantly reminded of how lucky I am to have such wonderful friends and family. Their support, encouragement, and, of course, their patience are what buoy me through the tough times and make the good times even better. I'm particularly grateful to my parents, Robert and Anne, whose gentle guidance and constant faith have allowed me to succeed, fail, and figure myself out. And to my amazing siblings, Charlotte, Isabelle, and Gordon—you guys have shaped me into the person I am today.

About the Author

Pippa Eccles Armbrester is a quiltmaker and designer whose work features bold geometric designs and bright solid colors. She began making quilts six years ago, and worked briefly in publishing after graduating from college, but soon decided to pursue her passion for patchwork full-time. She now sells her quilts online and in local stores, and often works on commission to create unique pieces suited to individual clients.

Aside from endless hours of quiltmaking, Pippa loves daily hot-yoga classes, biking around town, cooking, baking bread, knitting, and traveling. A day spent by the ocean, hours with a good book, or an evening over a delicious meal with a friend at a favorite restaurant are her little slices of heaven. She lives and works in Boston, her favorite city in the world, with her wonderful husband, Kyle (whose patience with the pins and needles scattered around the house is very much appreciated), and her tiny teacup poodle, Martin. Visit her online at pippapatchwork.com.